DISC

THE EVENTS *of*

THE SECOND COMING

> Mark,
> May the Holy Spirit empower you to be a Watchman to the body of Christ. Til Eternity
> Paul

PAUL BORTOLAZZO

Discovering the Events of the Second Coming
Copyright © 2018 by Paul Bortolazzo
All rights reserved.

No part of this publication may be reproduced, stored in a retrieval system or transmitted in any way by any means, electronic, mechanical, photocopy, recording or otherwise without the prior permission of the author except as provided by USA copyright law.

Scripture quotations marked "NKJV" are taken from The New King James Version / Thomas Nelson Publishers, Nashville: Thomas Nelson Publishers. Copyright © 1992. Used by permission. All rights reserved.

ISBN: 978-1722908164
ISBN: 1722908165
Also available in eBook
Publishing Assistant, The Author's Mentor
www.TheAuthorsMentor.com
Cover Design: Hyliian Graphics

PUBLISHED IN THE UNITED STATES OF AMERICA

Discovering the events Jesus will fulfill during His Second Coming is the key to understanding The Revelation of Jesus Christ.

Watchman Paul Bortolazzo

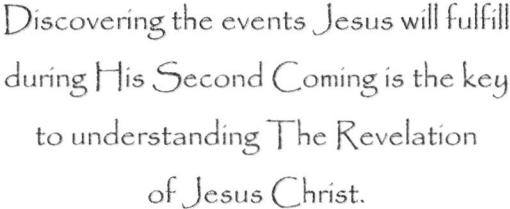

TABLE OF CONTENTS

The Promise of His Coming 1
The Wolves In Sheep's Clothing 7
The Coming Of Our Lord Jesus Christ 16
The Seventy Weeks Of Daniel 20
The Day Of The Lord 27
The Time Of The End 31

1. The Falling Away 35
2. A Little Horn 41
3. First Seal: The White Horse 43
4. He Will Confirm A Covenant 46
5. The Temple Of God 50
6. Second Seal: The Red Horse 52
7. The Great Harlot 54
8. Third Seal: The Black Horse 58
9. The Woman Having Twelve Stars 61
10. The Restrainer 63
11. A War In Heaven 65
12. The Beast 68
13. The False Prophet 72
14. Fourth Seal: The Pale Horse 75

15. The Great Tribulation: Satan's Wrath 78
16. The Two Witnesses 85
17. First Angel: Preaching The Gospel 87
18. Second Angel: Mystery Babylon Falls................90
19. Third Angel: Do Not Worship The Beast............ 91
20. Fifth Seal: Martyrdom 94
21. The Valley Of Jehoshaphat.................................. 96
22. Sixth Seal: Sun, Moon, and Stars....................... 98
23. The Sign Of The Son of Man............................. 102
24. The Coming Of The Son of Man 105
25. The Judgment Seat Of Christ 115
26. The 144,000 Sealed 123
27. Seventh Seal: Silence In Heaven 125
28. The Day Of The Lord's Wrath 127
29. First Trumpet: Hail And Fire............................ 131
30. Second Trumpet: A Sea Of Blood.....................133
31. Third Trumpet: Infected Rivers 135
32. Fourth Trumpet: A Third Of The Sun Struck 137
33. Fifth Trumpet: The Bottomless Pit 139
34. Sixth Trumpet: A Third Of Mankind Killed........ 141
35. The Death Of The Two Witnesses......................143

36. The Physical Return Of The Holy One 147
37. They Will Look On Me 154
38. I Will Gather The Remnant 158
39. The Mystery Of God 162
40. The Breath Of Life 165
41. The Lamb On Mount Zion 166
42. Seventh Trumpet: He Shall Reign 168
43. The Mount Of Olives Split 172
44. The Sea Of Glass 174
45. First Bowl: Loathsome Sores 176
46. Second Bowl: Sea Creatures Die 178
47. Third Bowl: Rivers Like Blood 179
48. Fourth Bowl: Scorched by Fire 181
49. Fifth Bowl: A Kingdom Of Darkness 182
50. Sixth Bowl: Kings From The East 183
51. Seventh Bowl: His Wrath Is Done 185
52. The Fate Of Babylon 187
53. The Marriage Of The Lamb 192
54. The Appearing Of The Word of God 193
55. The Mountain Of The Lord's House 198
56. A Remnant Will Return 200

57. I Will Gather All Nations 203
58. The Temple Of The Lord 204
59. Standing Before The Ancient Of Days 207
60. The Reign Of Christ 210
61. Satan In The Bottomless Pit 213
62. The Authority To Judge 215
63. The Resurrection Of Martyrs 217
64. A New Heaven And A New Earth 220
65. The Lamb And His Bride 224
66. The Throne Of God 228
67. Satan Released To Deceive 233
68. Tormented Forever 235
69. A Great White Throne 237
70. Then Comes The End 240

A Final Exhortation 242
Chart: The Seven Seals 253
Chart: The Second Coming Of Christ 254
Chart: The 70 Weeks of Daniel 255

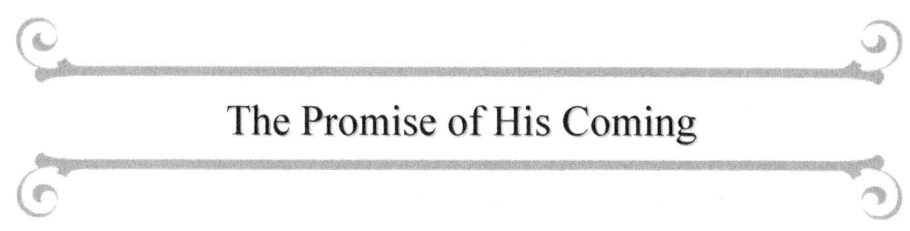

The Promise of His Coming

'Knowing this first: that scoffers will come in the last days, walking according to their own lusts, and saying, "Where is the promise of His coming? For since the fathers fell asleep, all things continue as they were from the beginning of creation." 2 Peter 3:3-4**

After becoming a Christian in 1975, I had lots of 'when' questions about the Second Coming of Christ.

When will the Son of Man gather His elect?
When will the Holy One finish the mystery of God?
When will the Word of God appear at Armageddon?
When will the Lamb of God return with His bride?

My pastor looked uneasy after I asked him these questions.

"Paul, no one knows when our Lord will come back. Studying end time events is a waste of time. You should be out winning souls."

"Then why did the disciples ask for the sign of His coming?"

"Son, Jesus will come for us when He wants to. Worrying about the future is not God's will. Sharing the gospel is the only thing that matters."

His reply sounded reasonable. Yet my questions wouldn't go away. My friends assured me God will bring an end to this world in His timing, not mine. My desire to understand didn't seem to matter. I tried rephrasing my questions. That didn't work either. I wondered why I couldn't get any answers. A close friend advised me not to be afraid. He said there are some things we will never know until we go to heaven. After a few more brush offs the conviction from the Holy Spirit faded away.

'... "These are the ones who come out of the great tribulation, and washed their robes and made them white in the blood of the Lamb." Revelation 7:14

A few years later, I was studying The Revelation of Jesus Christ. In his vision, John saw a great multitude in heaven. Blood bought believers from every nation have come out of the Great Tribulation and are standing before the throne of God. They're praising the Father and the Lamb for their salvation. I suddenly realized my desire to understand was never fueled by worry or fear about the future. *It was the Holy Spirit prompting me to discover the events Jesus will fulfill during His Second Coming.*

"And in vain they worship Me, teaching as doctrines the commandments of men." Matthew 15:9

'Since you have purified your souls in obeying the truth through the Spirit in sincere love of the brethren, love one another fervently with a pure heart.' 1 Peter 1:22

Many are convinced Jesus won't be returning in their lifetime. Driven by their lusts, they have become scoffers. So how can we expose this smokescreen from Satan? It begins with discipleship. God chose ministers for the equipping of the saints, for the work of the ministry. A critical truth of the Great Commission is our Lord coming back a second time. Every

Christian should be strengthened by this glorious truth. Then why are so many abandoning this promise? Why are pastors no longer teaching the consequences of the Second Coming? They're actually redefining His coming by the commandments of men. How else can you explain so many different interpretations? For some, obeying the truth through the Spirit is no longer a priority.

"He who has an ear, let him hear what the Spirit says to the churches." Revelation 2:29

Let me ask you some questions about the Second Coming.

What events will warn us His coming is near?
What event will initiate His coming?
What events will be fulfilled during His coming?
What event will complete His coming?
Do you know?

The fact is, the Holy Spirit is teaching these truths to any believer having an ear to hear.

'Now as He sat on the Mount of Olives opposite the temple, Peter, James, John, and Andrew asked Him privately... "Tell us...what will be the sign of Your coming...?" Mark 13:3-4

Just days before His crucifixion, Peter, James, John, and Andrew left the temple in Jerusalem and followed their Lord up to the Mount of Olives. Jesus had already told them His coming will be like the days of Noah and Lot. Their hearts were heavy. They could have asked many questions. The one they did ask was about His coming back. They wanted to know the sign of His coming (harvest).

"Therefore you also be ready, for the Son of Man is coming at an hour you do not expect." Luke 12:40

"So you also, when you see all these things, know that it is near-at the doors." Matthew 24:33

If our sins are washed away by His blood, then we're ready for heaven. We are not necessarily ready for His Second Coming. If being saved meant we're ready, then the warnings to watch and not be deceived would be meaningless. Jesus is coming back like a thief in the night. This is why He wants the body of Christ watching for the events warning His coming is near.

"Take heed that no one deceives you…" Matthew 24:4

'But evil men and impostors will grow worse and worse, deceiving and being deceived.' 2 Timothy 3:13

Jesus is exhorting us not to be deceived in these last days before His coming. Here are five deceptions evil imposters are using to deceive many believers.

'Blessed is he who reads and those who hear the words of this prophecy and keep those things which are written in it; for the time is near.' Revelation 1:3

"How can you keep the things written in this prophecy if no one agrees? Most pastors I know avoid The Book of Revelation."

'Little children, it is the last hour; and as you have heard that the Antichrist is coming, even now many antichrists have come, by which we know that it is the last hour.' 1 John 2:18

"Doomsayers are saying the Antichrist is coming, even though no such person exists. Their fear tactics won't work on me."

"I was watching; and the same horn was making war against the saints and prevailing against them." Daniel 7:21

"My God is love. No one will ever war or prevail over the saints. Stop listening to such fearmongering. It will never happen."

"For as in the days before the flood, they were eating and drinking, marrying and giving in marriage, until the day that Noah entered the ark, and did not know until the flood came and took them all away, so also will the coming of the Son of Man be." Matthew 24:38-39

"The coming of our Lord will be just like the days of Noah. The righteous were left and the wicked were taken away."

"If anyone takes away from the words of the book of this prophecy, God shall take away his part from the Book of Life, from the holy city, and from the things which are written in this book." Revelation 22:19

"My past, present, and future sins are forgiven. I possess eternal life. No one can take away my part in the Book of Life."

'Consider what I say, and may the Lord give you understanding in all things.' 2 Timothy 2:7

Understanding where the events of the last days fit in can be overwhelming. This is why so many have given up trying. So, I asked the Holy Spirit to teach me. The answer I received is the message of the hour to the church. The best way to understand is to study these events in chronological order. The Holy Spirit is teaching believers the future events that will take place before, during, and after the Second Coming of Christ. We will begin with the next event on His end-time calendar. Our goal is to study the last seventy events till the Son delivers the kingdom back to His Father. This way we can see the timing of each event, it's purpose, and how it relates to other events.

The Wolves In Sheep's Clothing

"Behold, I send you out as sheep in the midst of wolves. Therefore, be wise as serpents and harmless as doves." Matthew 10:16

In 1998, the Holy Spirit led me to create a new ministry. Understanding the events of the coming of our Lord Jesus Christ is for the equipping of the saints. I taught this truth in churches, in homes, and on the streets. It was exciting experiencing divine appointments created by the Holy Spirit. Yet the spiritual warfare I encountered was intense. I was shocked by so many who could care less. This shouldn't be too surprising when you study The Revelation of Jesus Christ. In the first century, John sent his letter to seven churches. **(Rev. 2:1-3:22)** What the apostle wrote down wasn't pretty. Some in these churches had lost their first love. Many were lukewarm. Others were dying spiritually. These sins are a prophetic picture of many living today. The fruit of such compromise is their lack of faith in His coming. **(Luke 18:8)**

"Then they will deliver you up to tribulation and kill you, and you will be hated by all nations for My name's sake...But he who endures to the end shall be saved." Matthew 24:9, 13

Most pastors admit we're living in the last days. Yet, they have no intention of making disciples capable of overcoming the severe persecution that is coming. **(Mat 24:9-13; 28:19-20)** Many prefer teaching on prosperity, inner healing, even financial planning. Such emphasis will never produce what Christians are really yearning for. Their focus has become a numbers game. How large is their sanctuary? How many are attending? How many are tithing? How big is their youth group? How good is their praise team? A major priority is to be positive and not judge. Such feel-good messages are producing the largest churches in the world. Make no mistake, such veiled rebellion gravitates toward pleasing man rather than God. **(Jam. 4:4)**

"If you were of the world, the world would love its own. Yet because you are not of the world, but I chose you out of the world, therefore the world hates you." John 15:19

For many years, the world has bombarded the church with the mantra, don't judge lest you be judged. **(Mat. 7:1)** Let us discern the demonic spirit using this ploy. The world hates anyone declaring the teachings of Jesus. The wicked will never embrace those righteously judging their rebellion. Is this why so many Christians are no longer willing to suffer for the sake of righteousness? **(John 15:19, John 7:24, 1 Pet. 3:14)**

'For what have I to do with judging those also who are outside? Do you not judge those who are inside?' 1 Corinthians 5:12

One of the most deceptive lies from Satan is we aren't to judge. Famous ministers are teaching that's the job of the Holy Spirit. Many are now convinced anyone exposing false teachers is somehow dividing the church. The truth is, our Lord is exhorting us to make a righteous judgment; not according to appearance. **(John 7:24)** Why are we seeing such a lack of repentance? More and more Christians are refusing to judge the evil behavior of those inside the church. **(1 Cor. 5:11-13)**

"Beware of false prophets, who come to you in sheep's clothing, but inwardly they are ravenous wolves." Matthew 7:15

In these last days before His coming, Jesus is warning us against false prophets pretending to be sheep but inwardly are ravenous wolves. **(Mat. 7:15; 10:16; 24:11)** We have all seen the horrific damage inflicted by these false teachers. **(2 Tim. 4:3)** Let's expose three destructive heresies popular wolves are using to deceive many believers. **(2 Pet. 2:1, Mat. 24:4-5)**

THE DENIAL OF THE SON OF GOD

'And the angel answered and said to her, "The Holy Spirit will come upon you, and the power of the Highest will overshadow you; therefore, also, that Holy One who is to be born will be called the Son of God." Luke 1:35

"And she will bring forth a Son, and you shall call His name JESUS, for He will save His people from their sins." Matthew 1:21

An angel said the Holy One that is to be born will be called the Son of God. Joseph and Mary were instructed to name Him, Jesus. **(Luke 1:35, Mat. 1:21)** He is Immanuel; God with us. The Word of God becoming flesh; the only begotten Son of the Father. **(John 1:1-14)** Recently, several wolves were boldly teaching Christians and Muslims worship the same God; even though they know Muslims don't believe God has a Son. Why is this so evil? The wrath of God abides on anyone denying Jesus as the only begotten Son of God. **(John 3:36)**

'He who has the Son has life; he who does not have the Son of God does not have life.' 1 John 5:12

This celebrated false prophet boldly declared the Holy Spirit gave him this new revelation. His TV audience was captivated when he shouted, "You don't have God in you; you are God." He insisted Christians are an exact replica of the Son of God! It was more than shocking when his audience began praising the Lord. This heresy is a blatant denial of the Son of God. **(John 3:18, 1 John 5:11-12)** Believers will never inherit divinity. There will always be one God; consisting of the Father, the Word, and the Holy Spirit. **(1 John 5:7)**

'He has delivered us from the power of darkness and conveyed us into the kingdom of the Son of His love, in whom we have redemption through His blood, the forgiveness of sins.' Colossian 1:13-14

'These things I have written to you who believe in the name of the Son of God, that you may know that you have eternal life, and that you may continue to believe in the name of the Son of God.' 1 John 5:13

This revered apostle raised his hands to quiet his packed-out congregation. He paused and shared, "When Jesus was on the cross, He became a sinner and died spiritually."

His evil assertion Jesus somehow became unholy is not possible. God is unchangeable. Jesus is the same yesterday, today, and forever. **(Mal. 3:6, Heb. 13:8)** The Son will never cease being divine. There is more. This pastor taught in order to defeat the Devil, Jesus had to suffer in hell for three days. Saints, the Son of Man triumphed over all principalities when He died on the cross. **(Col. 1:13-14, 1 John 5:13-20)** We have redemption only through His shed blood. To teach the Christ had to suffer in hell is blasphemy. Anyone believing such heresies is denying the Son of God. **(Col. 2:14-15, John 3:36)**

THE DENIAL OF THE LAKE OF FIRE

'And anyone not found written in the Book of Life was cast into the lake of fire.' Revelation 20:15

'Beloved, while I was very diligent to write to you concerning our common salvation, I found it necessary to write to you exhorting you to contend earnestly for the faith which was once for all delivered to the saints.' Jude 1:3

This well-known pastor once led a church of six thousand. The exodus began the Sunday he taught everyone will go to heaven. He now believes the lake of fire is symbolic. **(Rev. 20:15)** His congregation was willing to contend for the faith by exposing this lie from Satan. **(Jude 1:3)** They knew he was no longer abiding in the doctrine of Christ. **(John 1:9)** So they made a righteous judgment and left. **(John 7:24)** This pastor lost his church, his ministry, his reputation and his friends. Even so, God is still giving him time to repent so his spirit may be saved. **(1 Cor. 5:5)**

"And do not fear those who kill the body but cannot kill the soul. But rather fear Him who is able to destroy both soul and body in hell." Matthew 10:28

Many young adults are excited about steering Christianity in a new direction. Their emergent pastors are teaching them the lie God will never cast anyone into hell. Sadly, not many believe in Jesus as their Lord and Savior. We must enter into eternal life through a narrow gate. The path to heaven is so difficult; very few will find it. **(Acts 14:2, Mat. 7:13-14)** In the end, most will choose the broad gate leading to everlasting fire. **(Mat. 25:41, 46)** This is why we should not fear those who can kill the body. Instead, we should fear (respect) God; the only One able to destroy both soul and body in hell. **(Mat. 10:28)**

"But I say to you that whoever is angry with his brother without a cause shall be in danger of the judgment. And whoever says to his brother, 'Raca' shall be in danger of the council. But whoever says, 'You fool' shall be in danger of hell fire." Matthew 5:22

According to our Lord, anyone refusing to repent of such anger toward a brother will go to hell fire when they die. This isn't about calling someone foolish. It's about the condition of one's heart. Calling a brother, a fool is like saying they're worthless. You could care less if they're saved. Another example of being angry without a cause is, "You can fight the Antichrist if you want. I don't care. I'll be in heaven." For years I've heard Christians gleefully repeating this curse. They could care less about the destiny of those disagreeing with them. It's tough to hear such contempt. Such deep-seated anger is unacceptable because it's from deceiving spirits. **(Mat. 5:20-22, 1 Tim. 4:1)**

THE DENIAL OF THE RESURRECTION

'But there were also false prophets among the people, even as there will be false teachers among you, who will secretly bring in destructive heresies, even denying the Lord who bought them, and bring on themselves swift destruction.' 2 Peter 2:1

It's only getting worse. Many Christians are being deceived by false prophets denying the Lord who once bought them. The fate of anyone trusting in their heresies denying the Lord is swift destruction. **(2 Pet. 2:1)**

'Now, brethren, concerning the coming of our Lord Jesus Christ and our gathering together to Him, we ask you.' 2 Thessalonians 2:1

Today, there is a popular movement called the New Apostolic Reformation (Kingdom Now). This cult teaches the church must be restored to spiritual and physical dominance over Satan before our Lord can come back. I once heard a NAR prophet falsely prophesy the church isn't going anywhere. When he shouted Jesus isn't returning for a bruised-up bride the audience erupted in praise. He boldly declared the Son of Man isn't coming back until the church defeats Satan. Afterward, I interviewed several praising God for such an anointed message. Their lack of discernment was heartbreaking. They had no idea they just heard a false prophet denying the resurrection of the elect from the wrath to come! **(Rev. 7:9-17; 15:1)**

"No one can come to Me unless the Father who sent Me draws him; and I will raise him up at the last day." John 6:44

Preterist means past. They boldly teach in The Revelation of Jesus Christ have already happened. They're convinced the gathering of believers by angels took place in the first century.

Saints, this interpretation is not from the scriptures nor from the Holy Spirit. How so? Preterist's are denying the future resurrection of the elect on the last day. **(John 6:44; 11:24, Mat. 24:30-39)**

'And to wait for His Son from heaven, whom He raised from the dead, even Jesus who delivers us from the wrath to come.' 1 Thessalonians 1:10

The lack of accountability on TV is one of Satan's greatest tools. Wolves on TBN and DayStar are deceiving believers all over the world. A regular guest boldly teaches Jesus will deliver believers only after punishing the world for its evil. He insists the resurrection will take place just before Armageddon. **(Rev. 16:14-16)** Why is this so dangerous? **(Rev. 22:19)** These wolves are denying the promise by our Lord Jesus to deliver us from the wrath to come. **(1 Thes. 1:10, 2 Thes. 2:1, Mat. 24:29-39)**

'Whoever transgresses and does not abide in the doctrine of Christ does not have God. He who abides in the doctrine of Christ has both the Father and the Son." 2 John 1:9

In this chapter, there is a reason why the Holy Spirit led me to expose wolves denying the Son of God **(Rev. 2:18)**, denying the lake of fire **(Rev. 20:15)**, and denying the resurrection of the elect from the wrath to come. **(Rev. 7:9-17)** Only those continually abiding in the doctrine of Christ have God. In fact, we aren't to keep company with anyone professing Christ that is bringing a false doctrine. **(2 John 1:9-11)** Isn't this admonition a bit strong? Not when you consider the alternative. This is for our own protection lest we share in their evil deeds. **(1 Cor. 5:11-13, 2 Thes. 3:13-15)**

'These things I have written to you concerning those who try to deceive you.' I John 2:26

'And Jesus answered and said to them: "Take heed that no one deceives you. For many will come in My name, saying, 'I am the Christ,' and will deceive many." Matthew 24:4-5

"...Take heed that you not be deceived. For many will come in My name, saying, 'I am He,' and, 'The time has drawn near.' Therefore, do not go after them." Luke 21:8

In this late hour, there is another treacherous deception being sown by the enemy. Like an enormous Trojan horse from within; most are believing it without any question. What could it be? Many claiming to know Christ are declaring His coming is drawing near; at any moment. Jesus is warning us not to go after them! **(Mat. 24:4-5, Luke 21:8)**

The Coming Of Our Lord Jesus Christ

'Behold, He is coming with clouds, and every eye will see Him, even they who pierced Him. And all the tribes of the earth will mourn because of Him...' Revelation 1:7

While exiled to the Island of Patmos, the Alpha and Omega told John to write down The Revelation of Jesus Christ. **(Rev. 1:9-11)** Within his vision, the apostle saw the events Jesus will fulfill during His Second Coming. Understanding this prophetic letter is like fitting together pieces of a puzzle. May the Holy Spirit teach us the timing of these future events. **(Rev. 7:9-17; 10:1-7; 19:11-21; 21:9-10)**

"For as the lightning comes from the east and flashes to the west, so also will the coming of the Son of Man be." Matthew 24:27

As we draw closer to the harvest, the Holy Spirit is preparing a great multitude of overcomers from every nation. This divine preparation is based on the events the church will experience. You see, many are convinced the Second Coming is a single event. Sincere ministers are trying to fit the events Jesus will accomplish into one visit. Clearly, there is only one Second Coming. The scriptures speak of the coming, His coming, and Your coming. **(1 Thes. 4:15, 2 John 2:28, Mat. 24:3)** The misunderstanding is with the word coming. **(Mat. 24:27)**

"Then they will see the Son of Man coming in the clouds with great power and glory. And then He will send His angels, and gather together His elect from the four winds, from the farthest part of earth to the farthest part of heaven." Mark 13:26-27

Coming is an arrival with an ongoing presence. This includes the events Jesus will accomplish. While on the Mount of Olives, our Lord shared the event that will initiate His Second Coming. At His coming, angels will gather together His elect from heaven then earth. **(1 Thes. 4:13-17)** What do you mean? What if I told you His Second Coming is more than a single visit. Would you believe it? Probably not. On a typical Sunday morning, you will hear the gathering of believers is not His Second Coming. So, if the gathering of believers at His Coming isn't part of His Second Coming, then what is it? **(Mark 13:26-27, Luke 21:27-28)**

'But each one in his own order: Christ the firstfruits, afterward those who are Christ's at His coming.' 1 Corinthians 15:23

This is an illustration of His coming. Let's say I was invited to preach at a church in Nashville. I arrived on Friday and taught an evening session. The next day I taught a morning session. That afternoon I taped a radio show. Before returning home, I preached two services on Sunday. My coming to Nashville included everything I did while I was there. The same can be said for the events Jesus will fulfill during His Second Coming.

What did Jesus fulfill during His First Coming?

The Holy One was born in a manger. **(Luke 1:35; 2:16)**
The Word of God shared with teachers. **(Luke 2:46, Rev. 19:13)**
The Lamb of God was baptized. **(John 1:29, Mat. 3:13-16)**

The Son of Man saved the lost. **(Mat. 18:11, Luke 19:10)**
The Christ died on the cross for our sins. **(John 1:41, Cor. 15:3)**
The Son of God returned to His Father. **(John 20:17, Mark 16:19)**

What will Jesus fulfill during His Second Coming?

The coming of the Son of Man. **(Rev. 7:9-17)**
The physical return of the Holy One. **(Rev. 10:1-7)**
The appearing of the Word of God. **(Rev. 19:11-21)**
The return of the Lamb of God. **(Rev. 21:9-10)**

What will the Son of Man accomplish?

"Then they will see the Son of Man coming in the clouds with great power and glory. And then He will send His angels, and gather together His elect from the four winds, from the farthest part of earth to the farthest part of heaven" Mark 13:26-27

Jesus coming in great power and glory will initiate His Second Coming. **(Luke 21:27)** The Son of Man will send forth His angels at the sound of a great trumpet. **(Mat. 24:30-31)** They will gather together His elect from heaven then earth. **(Mark 13:26-27)**

What will the Holy One accomplish?

'But in the days of the sounding of the seventh angel, when he is about to sound, the mystery of God would be finished, as He declared to His servants the prophets.' Revelation 10:7

Jesus will physically return a second time to finish the mystery of God; the salvation of a remnant from Israel. **(Rev. 10:7, Heb. 9:28, Dan. 9:24, Rom. 11:25-27)** When Jewish believers see Jesus they will cry out, 'barukh haba b'shem Adonai' (blessed is He who comes in the name of the Lord). **(Mat. 23:37-39, Luke 1:35)**

What will the Word of God accomplish?

'Now I saw heaven opened, and behold, a white horse. And He who sat on him was called Faithful and True, and in righteousness He judges and makes war...His name is called The Word of God.' Revelation 19:11-13

Jesus will appear in heaven on the great day of God Almighty, Armageddon. During the supper of the great God, the Beast and False Prophet will be cast alive into the lake of fire. Then the Word of God will kill their followers. **(Rev. 16:14-16; 19:11-21)**

What will the Lamb of God accomplish?

"Come, I will show you the bride, the Lamb's wife." And he carried me away in the Spirit to a great and high mountain, and showed me the great city, the holy Jerusalem, descending out of heaven from God.' Revelation 21:9-10

Jesus will descend within a new heaven to a new earth on the first day of His reign over the nations. The Lamb of God and His bride will rule for a thousand years from inside the holy Jerusalem. **(Rev. 21:9-10; 20:6)**

The Seventy Weeks Of Daniel

'And he informed me, and talked with me, and said, "O Daniel, I have now come forth to give you skill to understand." Daniel 9:22

'Seventy weeks are determined for your people and for your holy city, to finish the transgression, to make an end of sins, to make reconciliation for iniquity, to bring in everlasting righteousness, to seal up vision and prophecy, and to anoint the Most Holy.' Daniel 9:24

What end time prophecy did Daniel receive from an angel? God sent Gabriel predicting the fulfillment of the Christ's First and Second Coming. May the Holy Spirit teach us this prophecy called the Seventy Weeks of Daniel. **(Dan. 9:22-27)**

'And the LORD has sent to you all His servants the prophets, rising early and sending them, but you have not listened nor inclined your ear to hear.' Jeremiah 25:4

Who refused to listen to the prophets sent by God? During the evil rule of Jehoiakim, the worship of other gods kindled the anger of the Lord. **(Jer. 25:1-10)** The refusal by the children of Judah to listen to the prophets brought forth God's judgment. **(Jer. 25:4)**

"I will send and take all the families of the north," says the LORD, 'and Nebuchadnezzar the king of Babylon, My servant, and will bring them against this land, against its inhabitants, and against these nations...and will utterly destroy them..."' Jeremiah 25:9

In 606 B.C., King Nebuchadnezzar conquered Jerusalem. His armies brought noble captives back to Babylon. Among them was a teenager named Daniel. His name means, 'God is my judge'. Because of Daniel's faithfulness, Nebuchadnezzar promoted him ruler over the province of Babylon and chief administrator of all the wise men. **(Dan. 2:48)** Regretfully, the same could not be said about the Jewish people left behind in Jerusalem. **(Jer. 25:1-11)**

'In the first year of his reign I, Daniel, understood by the books the number of the years specified by the word of the LORD through Jeremiah the prophet, that He would accomplish seventy years in the desolations of Jerusalem.' Daniel 9:2

Jeremiah prophesied the children of Judah would serve the King of Babylon for seventy years. Nebuchadnezzar's rule over Judah began in 606 B.C. It ended when the Medo-Persians conquered Babylon in 536 B.C. **(Dan. 9:2)**

'And this whole land shall be a desolation and an astonishment, and these nations shall serve the king of Babylon seventy years.' Jeremiah 25:11

In 538 B.C., Daniel knew the captivity of his people would end in less than two years. Most had lost any hope of God restoring their beloved city. **(Jer. 25:11)** The prophet knew the curses from the Law of Moses were being poured out. This divine judgment would only get worse if Israel continued to disobey. In this dark hour, Daniel pleaded with God to turn away His anger from Jerusalem. He beseeches the Lord to shine His face on His desolate sanctuary and not delay their deliverance. **(Dan. 9:11-19)**

'Now while I was speaking, praying, and confessing my sin and the sin of my people Israel, and presenting my supplication before the LORD my God...yes, while I was speaking in prayer, the man Gabriel, whom I had seen in the vision at the beginning, being caused to fly swiftly, reached me about the time of the evening offering.' Daniel 9:20-21

While Daniel was confessing the sins of his people and asking for forgiveness, the Lord sent an angel. During the time of the evening offering, Gabriel arrived with a word concerning the future of Israel. Because of their refusal to repent, God decreed a future chastisement of Daniel's people. **(Dan. 9:20-21)** Let's study the events of the prophecy the angel told the prophet.

'That from the going forth of the command to restore and build Jerusalem until Messiah the Prince, there shall be seven weeks and sixty-two weeks; The street shall be built again, and the wall, Even in troublesome times. And after the sixty-two weeks Messiah shall be cut off...' Daniel 9:25-26

This prophecy began with the death of the Messiah. The angel Gabriel predicted the Messiah would be cut off after the children of Israel suffer sixty-nine weeks of Gentile persecution. This persecution began after Artaxerxes gave the prophet Nehemiah the command to restore the gates of the temple and the wall of Jerusalem. **(Neh. 2:5-8)** Four hundred and eighty-three years later, Jesus was crucified on Passover. The angel foretold the day the Lamb gave His life for our sins. **(Mark 15:25-34)** This was the first event of Gabriel's prophecy. **(Dan. 9:25-26a)**

'...And the people of the prince who is to come shall destroy the city and the sanctuary.' Daniel 9:26b

Before the 70th week of Daniel can begin, Gabriel prophesied the destruction of the city and the sanctuary. In 70 A.D., Titus led his Roman armies into Jerusalem and overwhelmed the people. Over one million Jews died. Their temple was destroyed. Our Lord correctly predicted not one stone would be left upon another. **(Luke 19:43-44)** Because of their rebellion, God scattered the children of Israel throughout the earth. This is called the Great Diaspora. **(Lev. 26:33, Deut. 28:64-65)** This was the second event of Gabriel's prophecy. **(Dan. 9:26b)**

'And the ten horns that were on its head, and the other horn which came up, before which three fell, namely, that horn which had eyes and a mouth which spoke pompous words, whose appearance was greater than his fellows.' Daniel 7:20

'Then he shall confirm a covenant with many for one week...' Daniel 9:27a

The next event will initiate the 70th week of Daniel. It will begin when the Little Horn (Beast) confirms a covenant between Israel and her surrounding enemies for one week (seven years). **(Dan. 9:27a)** For the first half of the 70th week (3 ½ years), the Jewish people will be living in peace. **(Ezek. 38:1-14, Psa. 83)** This is the third event of Gabriel's prophecy. **(Dan. 9:27a)**

'...But in the middle of the week He shall bring an end to sacrifice and offering. And on the wing of abominations shall be one who makes desolate...' Daniel 9:27b

In the middle of the 70th week, the Beast will break this covenant by invading an unsuspecting Jerusalem with his armies. **(Rev. 17:12-13, Ezek. 38:1-14)** He will become the abomination who brings desolation to the holy place. **(Mat. 24:15, Luke 21:20)** This is the fourth event of Gabriel's prophecy. **(Dan. 9:27b)**

'Seventy weeks are determined For your people and for your holy city, To finish the transgression, To make an end of sins, To make reconciliation for iniquity, To bring in everlasting righteousness, To seal up vision and prophecy, And to anoint the Most Holy.' Daniel 9:24

Gabriel predicted the day the Most Holy will return a second time for the salvation of Israel. **(Luke 1:35, Dan. 9:24)** Before the Lord can bring in everlasting righteousness, Israel must suffer 490 years (70 weeks) of Gentile persecution. Sixty-nine weeks were fulfilled when Jesus died on the cross. **(Dan. 9:25-26)** There is still a seven-year week left before the Holy One returns to complete the mystery of God. **(Heb. 9:28, Rev. 10:1-7)** This is the fifth event of Gabriel's prophecy. **(Dan. 9:24, Rom. 11:25-27)**

'Although I heard, I did not understand. Then I said, "My lord, what shall be the end of these things?" And he said, "Go your way, Daniel, for the words are closed up and sealed till the time of the end." Daniel 12:9

After hearing all five events from the angel, Daniel still didn't understand. That's because the words of this prophecy are sealed up till the time of the end. Discerning the last three events is for those experiencing the 70th week of Daniel. Let's review the events Gabriel described to Daniel. **(Dan. 12:9)**

First Event-Gabriel predicted the very day the Messiah was killed. There were 69 weeks from the order to rebuild the gates of the temple in Jerusalem till His death. At the end of 483 years, Jesus was crucified on Passover. **(Dan. 9:25-26)**

Second Event-In 70 A.D., Roman armies destroyed Jerusalem. Because of their blatant disobedience, God scattered the Jewish people among the nations. This is called the Great Diaspora. **(Dan. 9:26, Luke 19:43-44, Neh. 1:8, Deut. 28:64-65)**

Third Event-The 70th week will begin after the Little Horn (Beast) confirms a seven-year covenant with Israel and her Muslim neighbors. In the first half of the week, the Jewish people will be living in peace with her enemies. **(Dan. 9:27a, Ezek. 38:11-14)**

Fourth Event-In the middle of the 70th week, the Abomination of Desolation (Beast) and his armies from ten nations will break this covenant by invading an unsuspecting Jerusalem. **(Dan. 9:27, Mat. 24:15, Luke 21:20, Rev. 17:12-13, Ezek. 38:1-12)**

Fifth Event- From the decree to rebuild Jerusalem, the Jewish people will suffer seventy weeks of Gentile domination (490 years). This event will complete the 70th week. At the end of this seven-year week, the Holy One will physically return and save a remnant from Israel. **(Dan. 9:24, Rom. 11:25-27, Rev. 10:1-7)**

'So Christ was once offered to bear the sins of many; and unto them that look for him shall he appear the second time without sin unto salvation.' Hebrews 9:28

The 70th Week of Daniel prophecy involves the First and Second Coming of Christ. **(Dan. 9:24-27)**

During His First Coming, at the end of the 69th week, the Messiah was crucified for the sins of the world. **(Dan. 9:25-26, Mark 15:20-34)**

During His Second Coming, at the end of the 70th week, the Most Holy will physically return a second time for the salvation of Israel. **(Dan. 9:24, Heb. 9:28, Rom. 11:25-27, Rev. 10:1-7)**

Many don't believe in a 2,000-year gap of time between the 69th and 70th weeks. They insist the 70th week was fulfilled in the first century. Why is this not possible? It's because the Second Coming is still future. **(Rev. 7:9-17; 10:1-7; 19:11-21; 21:9-10)**

"Therefore when you see the 'abomination of desolation,' spoken of by Daniel the prophet, standing in the holy place" (whoever reads, let him understand)." Matthew 24:15

While atop the Mount of Olives, Jesus warned His disciples of a critical event that will take place during the 70th week of Daniel. **(Dan. 9:27)** What exactly will happen when the Abomination of Desolation stands in the holy place in Jerusalem? **(Mat. 24:15-22)** When asked this question, most admit they have never been taught this prophecy. The truth is, our Lord wants everyone to understand the timing and consequences of the events Gabriel told Daniel. **(Dan. 9:24-27)**

The Day Of The Lord

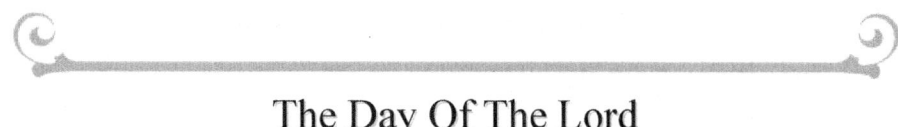

'**The sun shall be turned into darkness, and the moon into blood, before the coming of the great and awesome day of the Lord.' Joel 2:31**

The Day of the Lord is mentioned more in scripture than any other event. Since 1998, I've asked thousands of Christians what is the great and awesome Day of the Lord? I rarely received a right answer. Let's see how Old Testament prophets define it.

'**For this is the day of the Lord GOD of hosts, a day of vengeance, that He may avenge Himself on His adversaries ...' Jeremiah 46:10**

Jeremiah predicted the Lord will avenge His adversaries.

"**The day is coming, burning like an oven...all who do wickedly will be stubble. And the day which is coming shall burn them up," says the LORD of hosts.' Malachi 4:1**

Malachi prophesied the wicked will be burned up.

'**...For the day of the Lord is great and very terrible; who can endure it?' Joel 2:11**

Joel reflected who can endure this terrible day of wrath.

'Woe to you who desire the day of the LORD. For what good is the day of the LORD to you? It will be darkness, and not light.' Amos 5:18

Amos rebuked those desiring the Lord to punish their enemies.

'You should not have stood at the crossroads to cut off those among them who escaped; nor should you have delivered up those...who remained in the day of distress...Your reprisal shall return upon your own head.' Obadiah 1:14-15b

Obadiah warned against cutting off those trying to escape.

'Seek the LORD, all...who have upheld His justice. Seek righteousness, seek humility. It may be that you will be hidden in the day of the Lord's anger.' Zephaniah 1:7

Zephaniah saw believers hidden in the day of the Lord's anger.

'Behold, the day of the Lord comes, Cruel, with both wrath and fierce anger, to lay the land desolate; And He will destroy its sinners from it.' Isaiah 13:9

What do the apostles call this destruction of sinners? **(Isa. 13:9)** Paul calls it the day of Christ **(2 Thes. 2:2)**, in the day of the Lord Jesus Christ **(2 Cor. 1:14)**, the day of the Lord Jesus **(1 Cor. 5:5)**, the day of Jesus Christ **(Phil. 1:6)**, and the day of the Lord **(1 Thes. 5:2)**. Peter calls this day of wrath, the day of the Lord **(2 Pet. 3:10)**, the day of God **(2 Pet. 3:12)** and the day of judgment **(2 Pet. 2:9)**.

'But the day of the Lord will come as a thief in the night, in which the heavens will pass away with a great noise, and the elements will melt with fervent heat; both the earth and the works that are in it will be burned up.' 2 Peter 3:10

'I will bring the one–third through the fire, will refine them as silver is refined, and test them as gold is tested. They will call on My name, And I will answer them...' Zechariah 13:9

The Day of the Lord has a twofold purpose. During this judgment by God, heaven and earth will be dissolved by fire. This will result in a new heaven and a new earth in which righteousness dwells. **(2 Pet. 3:10-12)** The second purpose is the salvation of Jews calling on the name of the Lord. **(Zech. 13:9, Mat. 23:39)**

'I will cleanse them from all their iniquity by which they have sinned against Me...' Jeremiah 33:8

When will the Lord cleanse Israel of her iniquity? At the end of the 70th Week of Daniel, the Christ will physically return a second time. Those believing in the Holy One will be spiritually and physically saved. **(Dan. 9:24, Heb. 9:28, Rev. 10:1-7)**

'Not forsaking the assembling of ourselves together, as is the manner of some, but exhorting one another, and so much the more as you see the Day approaching.' Hebrews 10:25

Paul is urging believers not to forsake assembling together as we see this Day approaching. **(Heb. 10:25, 1 Thes. 5:2)** So if this Day is coming as a thief, then how can we see it approaching? **(Rev. 3:3)** God will punish the wicked the same day the Son of Man is revealed. **(Luke 17:26-30, Isa. 13:9-11)** Believers watching for the events warning us His coming is near will be ready. **(Mat. 24:3-33)**

'Looking for and hastening the coming of the day of God, because of which the heavens will be dissolved, being on fire, and the elements will melt with fervent heat?' 2 Peter 3:12

Every year environmentalists warn if global warming is not dealt with the extinction of plant species is unavoidable. As this debate drags on, I'm reminded of God's promise to never flood the earth again. **(Gen. 9:13-16)** He never will. The next time the wicked are judged it will be by fire. It's called the Day of the Lord. **(2 Pet. 3:12)**

The Time Of The End

'And he said, "Go your way, Daniel, for the words are closed up and sealed till THE TIME OF THE END." Daniel 12:9**

'Speak to the children of Israel, and say to them, "The feasts of the Lord, which you shall proclaim to be holy convocations, these are My feasts." Leviticus 23:2

The Feasts of The Lord are the redemptive career of the Messiah. Moses was told to proclaim all seven. Each Feast is an appointed time when God will meet with believers. Only by understanding the purpose of these holy convocations can one understand the fulfillment of the First and Second Coming of Christ. **(Lev. 23:1-44)**

'...That Christ died for our sins according to the Scriptures, and that He was buried, and that He rose again the third day...' 1 Corinthians 15:3-4

Jesus fulfilled the first four Feasts during His First Coming. **(Lev. 23:5-22, 1 Cor. 15:3-4)**

The Feast of Passover represents the shedding of His blood for the sins of the world. **(1 Pet. 1:19, 1 John 2:1-2, Isa. 53:4-6)**

The Feast of Unleavened Bread represents His body not decaying in the grave. **(Psa. 16:10, Acts 2:31)**

The Feast of Firstfruits represents His physical resurrection on the third day. **(1 Cor. 15:3-4, Luke 24:7)**

The Feast of Weeks (Pentecost) represents believers being baptized in the Holy Spirit. **(Acts 1:5; 2:4)**

'For the Lord Himself will descend from heaven with a shout, with the voice of an archangel, and with the trumpet of God...' 1 Thessalonians 4:16

Although you hardly ever hear this truth taught, which is why it's so hard for many to believe, Jesus will fulfill the last three Feasts of the Lord during His 2nd coming.

During the Feast of Trumpets (Rosh Hashanah), the Son of Man will gather His elect before pouring out His wrath upon the wicked. **(Lev. 23:24-25, Mat. 24:37-40)**

During the Day of Atonement (Yom Kippur), the Holy One will physically return for the salvation of Israel. **(Lev. 23:27-32, Dan. 9:24, Rom. 11:25-27, Heb. 9:28, Rev. 10:1-7)**

During the Feast of Tabernacles (Sukkot), the Lamb of God will gather His firstfruits before His final wrath destroys the wicked. **(Lev. 23:34-43, Rev. 14:1-4; 15:1; 16:17)**

'I say then, have they stumbled that they should fall? Certainly not. But through their fall, to provoke them to jealousy, salvation has come to the Gentiles.' Romans 11:11

After the Jews rejected their Messiah, the Gentiles became children of God by believing in Jesus as their Savior. Within the body of Christ, there is no distinction between a Jew and a Gentile. **(Rom. 11:11; 10:12)** Yet, the church hasn't replaced the children of Israel in their covenant relationship with God. Even though they wandered among the nations for many years, their blindness to the gospel is not permanent. **(Deut. 28:64-65, Rom. 11:25-27)** The covenant Abraham cut with God was never intended to guarantee salvation for all Jewish people. **(Gen. 17:1-7)** It did provide salvation for a remnant in every generation till the Holy One returns. **(Dan. 9:24, Rev.10:1-7)**

"O Jerusalem, Jerusalem, the one who kills the prophets and stones those who are sent to her. How often I wanted to gather your children together...but you were not willing." Matthew 23:37

In the first century, the children of Israel were scattered around the world because they refused to obey the voice of God. **(Deut. 28:62-66)** By the fourth century, Jerusalem was abandoned. The judgment of the Jewish people appeared to be final. The critical difference between Christianity and Judaism is sobering. The body of Christ believes Jesus is the only begotten Son of God. Judaism rejects Yeshua as the Son of God and is condemned for it. **(John 3:16,18)** Because of this, some ministers are teaching the promises given to Israel are now for the church. For many, physical Israel has disappeared from Bible prophecy. Such spiritualizing has only helped promote the persecution of the Jewish people. The Holocaust was proof enough. This genocide was an attempt by Satan to destroy Israel. Praise God, our Father has other plans for those believing in His Son. **(Mat. 23:37-39, Rom. 1:3; 11:25-27)**

"Who has heard such a thing? Who has seen such things? Shall the earth be made to give birth in one day? Or shall a nation be born at once? For as soon as Zion was in labor, She gave birth to her children." Isaiah 66:8

On May 14, 1948, Israel became a nation. On that day God fulfilled His promise to made her a nation again. **(Isa. 66:8)** Since her rebirth, millions have been gathered back to Zion. They represent the dry bones returning in unbelief just like the prophets predicted. **(Ezek. 37:21; 39:27-29)** Modern day Israel can be traced back to biblical times by her religion, her language, her prayers, her traditions, and her land. Her physical restoration cannot be denied. **(Zep. 3:20)**

'And the gospel must first be preached to all the nations.' Mark 13:10

The gospel must first be preached to all nations before our gathering at the coming of the Son of Man. **(Mark 13:10, 26-27, Rev. 14:6-7)** This is why understanding the timing and fulfillment of the last three Feasts is so critical. But, Paul, most pastors insist only the gospel matters. My friends, when you discover the consequences of the Feast of Trumpets, the Day of Atonement, and the Feast of Tabernacles you will be amazed how much it matters!

1. The Falling Away

'Though He was a Son, yet He learned obedience by the things which He suffered. And having been perfected, He became the author of eternal salvation to all who obey Him.' Hebrews 5:8-9

'Who shall bring a charge against God's elect?' Romans 8:33

Who is God's elect? Elect means 'chosen out'. One is elected by the author of eternal salvation, the Son of God. **(Heb. 5:8-9, 1 John 5:11-13)** In the New Testament, the elect are called the children of God **(1 John 3:1)**, brethren **(Heb. 3:12)**, sons of the light and day **(1 Thes. 5:5)**, overcomers **(Rev. 2:26)**, servants **(Rev. 19:5)** and saints **(Rev. 14:12)**.

"...The Holy Spirit, whom the Father will send in My name, He will teach you all things, and bring to your remembrance all things that I said to you." John 14:26

'Whoever transgresses and does not abide in the doctrine of Christ does not have God. He who abides in the doctrine of Christ has both the Father and the Son.' 2 John 1:9

The night I was born again, I asked Jesus to forgive me of all my sins. I believed in His death, burial, and resurrection. The Son of God became my Lord and Savior. **(Heb. 3:7, 1 John 2:27)** The Father sent the Holy Spirit to teach believers all things; bringing to remembrance everything Jesus taught. **(John 14:26)** The Holy Spirit is now my teacher. As I studied and prayed for understanding He taught me the doctrine of Christ. Which is the Gospel **(1 Cor. 15:1-4)**, the Virgin Birth **(Luke 1:35)**, the Trinity **(1**

John 5:7), the Promise of the Father (Acts 1:4-5), the gifts of the Holy Spirit (Heb. 2:4), the Feasts of the Lord (Lev. 23:2), the Coming of our Lord Jesus Christ (2 Thes. 2:1), the Resurrection of the righteous and unrighteous (John 5:28-29, Mark 13:26-27), and the Lake of Fire for the wicked. (Rev. 20:11-15). What really struck me was the witness I received after understanding these tenets of Christianity. Once learned, these truths are not optional. Beware saints, only those abiding in the doctrine of Christ have the Father and the Son. Those transgressing by no longer abiding do not have God. (2 John 1:9-10, 2 Pet. 2:1)

'Behold what manner of love the Father has bestowed on us, that we should be called children of God. Therefore the world does not know us, because it did not know Him.' 1 John 3:1

At this National Day of Prayer, a Jewish rabbi declared all faiths are equal. Seeing Christians applauding such blasphemy was painful. A person is either righteous or wicked. By His obedience, Jesus made many righteous. (Rom. 5:19) Those believing in the Son of God have everlasting life. (John 3:16) Those not believing are condemned. (John 3:18) Before the Son saved me, I was wicked. Jesus now sees me as a child of God. (1 John 3:1)

'Now the Spirit expressly says that in latter times some will depart from the faith, giving heed to deceiving spirits and doctrines of demons.' 1 Timothy 4:1

We are living in perilous times. Popular ministers having a form of godliness are flourishing. Due to the deceitfulness of sin, the conviction to repent is being ignored. (Heb. 3:12-13, Rev. 2:5) Believers are departing from the faith by giving heed to deceiving spirits and doctrines of demons. The greatest falling away in history is upon us. (I Tim. 4:1, 2 Thes. 2:3, Tim. 3:1-5)

'Beloved, do not believe every spirit, but test the spirits, whether they are of God; because many false prophets have gone out into the world.' I John 4:1

'In flaming fire taking vengeance on those who do not know God, and on those who do not obey the gospel of our Lord Jesus Christ.' 2 Thessalonians 1:8

This pastor leads the largest congregation in America. When asked if other religions are wrong for not believing in Jesus, he shamelessly claims they aren't. **(Jude 1:4)** He cites Hinduism as an example. He believes Hindus have a love for God. What God is he talking about? Hindus worship cows and rats. A person's love for a pagan religion will never make it true. **(Mat. 23:15)** Hinduism is a doctrine of demons leading billions to hell fire. **(Mat. 10:28)** The gospel is the death, burial, and resurrection. **(1 Cor. 15:3-4)** Beware saints, those not obeying the gospel of our Lord Jesus Christ are no longer saved. **(2 Thes. 1:8)**

'Then you shall again discern between the righteous and the wicked, between one who serves God and one who does not serve Him.' Malachi 3:18

Why are so many no longer willing to discern (judge) between the righteous and the wicked? Between those serving God and those who aren't? It's because they're lusting after the approval of man. No one can be a man pleaser and serve Christ at the same time. **(Mal. 3:18, 1 Pet. 4:1-2, 1 Gal. 1:10)**

'For the time will come when they will not endure sound doctrine, but according to their own desires, because they have itching ears, they will heap up for themselves teachers; and they will turn their ears away from the truth...' 2 Timothy 4:3-4

For many claiming Christ, enduring sound doctrine is no longer needed. Their selfish desires have opened a door for false teachers to give them what their itching ears want to hear. **(2 Tim. 4:3-4)** They're being offered the lust of the flesh, the lust of the eyes, and the pride of life. **(1 John 2:16)** Those turning away from the truth are no longer abiding in the doctrine of Christ. **(2 John 1:9)**

'For the message of the cross is foolishness to those who are perishing, but to us who are being saved it is the power of God.' 1 Corinthians 1:18

The message of the cross is foolishness to one of the most influential women in the world. Her brilliantly packaged mysticism is offering a false gospel. This celebrity assures her television audience Jesus did not come to earth to die on a cross for our sins. Rather, He came to give everyone a Christ consciousness. **(1 Cor. 1:18)**

"Let the Christ, the King of Israel, descend now from the cross, that we may see and believe." Even those who were crucified with Him reviled Him.' Mark 15:32

In Israel, the first hour of a day begins at six. It was nine in the morning when a soldier nailed His hands and feet to a wooden cross. Six hours later, He cried out it is done and physically died. That afternoon His body was buried in an empty tomb. Two days later, Jesus physically rose from the dead. No one would have ever been saved unless the Lamb of God gave His life for the sins of the world. The message of the cross is foolishness to those perishing. **(Mark 15:25-46, Luke 24:46, John 1:29)**

'For if he who comes preaches another Jesus whom we have not preached, or if you receive a different spirit which you have not received, or a different gospel which you have not accepted—you may well put up with it.' 1 Corinthians 11:4

This esteemed superstar claims there are many paths to heaven. She challenges her listeners not to embrace a specific belief about God. That God is a feeling experience. Make no mistake, Satan is using her to introduce another Jesus, a different Holy Spirit, and a different gospel. Due to their carnal desires, her supporters are rejecting the conviction of the Holy Spirit. This is why they're no longer discerning the demonic manipulation they're engaged in. **(1 Cor. 11:4, 2 Pet. 2:1, I John 3:7)**

'In this the children of God and the children of the devil are manifest: Whoever does not practice righteousness is not of God, nor is he who does not love his brother.' I John 3:10

Practicing righteousness is the difference between the children of God and the children of the Devil. Paul is exhorting us to be led by the Holy Spirit. Those who do won't be controlled by the lusts of their flesh. Clearly, anyone refusing to repent of their sins will not inherit the kingdom of God. **(1 John 3:10, Rom. 13:14, Gal. 5:21)**

'For if, after they have escaped the pollutions of the world through the knowledge of the Lord and Savior Jesus Christ, they are again entangled in them and overcome, the latter end is worse for them than the beginning.' 2 Peter 2:20

The only way to escape the pollutions of this world is by believing in Jesus as your Lord and Savior. Peter is warning believers not to go back and be entangled in the world. It's better not to have known the way of righteousness than to be saved and fall away. It's like a dog going back to its vomit. **(2 Pet. 2:20-22, Heb. 6:4-6)**

'Beware, brethren, lest there be in any of you an evil heart of unbelief in departing from the living God; but exhort one another daily, while it is called, "Today," lest any of you be hardened through the deceitfulness of sin.' Hebrews 3:12-13

Have you ever had friends forsake their Lord after yielding to an evil heart of unbelief? **(Heb. 3:12-13)** I have. What is going to happen to those hardened by the deceitfulness of sin? Sadly, anyone denying the Son before men, He will deny before His Father. **(Mat. 10:3)**

2. A Little Horn

> Due to their deceitfulness of sin, their love for Christ is gone. No longer capable of enduring sound doctrine, wolves are giving them what their itching ears want to hear. Obedience to the Spirit is never mentioned. The greatest apostasy is growing.

'Then he opened his mouth in blasphemy against God, to blaspheme His name, His tabernacle, and those who dwell in heaven.' Revelation 13:6

Who will speak pompous words and blasphemy against God? Daniel calls him the Little Horn. **(Dan. 7:8, 20-25)** John calls him the Beast. **(Rev. 13:2-7)** Paul calls him the Man of Sin, the Son of Perdition, and the Lawless One. **(2 Thes. 2:3, 8)** Our Lord calls him the one who makes desolate; the Abomination of Desolation. **(Mat. 24:15, Mark 13:14)** Because this deceiver will blaspheme Jesus the Christ, many will call him the Antichrist. **(1 John 2:18)**

'And I saw a beast rising up out of the sea, having seven heads and ten horns, and on his horns ten crowns, and on his heads a blasphemous name.' Revelation 13:1

"The ten horns which you saw are ten kings who have received no kingdom as yet, but they receive authority for one hour as kings with the beast. These are of one mind, and they will give their power and authority to the beast." Revelation 17:12-13

John saw the Beast rising to power having seven heads and ten horns. A blasphemous name is written on each head. **(Rev. 13:1)** The ten horns represent the leaders of ten nations who will give their power and authority to the Beast. **(Rev 17:12-13)**

"I was considering the horns, and there was another horn, a little one, coming up among them, before whom three of the first horns were plucked out by the roots. And there, in this horn, *were* eyes like the eyes of a man, and a mouth speaking pompous words." Daniel 7:8

What is next on Gods end time calendar? Before the 70th week of Daniel can begin; a pompous tyrant called the Little Horn (Beast) will physically subdue three Muslim nations. **(Dan. 7:7-8)** After this, he will convince seven more nations to give him their power and authority. **(Dan. 7:20-25, Rev. 17:12-13)** This power play has nothing to do with fighting Islamic terrorism. The Beast is going to force these ten nations (horns) to lay down their weapons and allow Israel to live in peace. **(Ezek. 38:11-14)**

3. First Seal: The White Horse

> The Little Horn is counting on the world's distrust of Islam. Most approve of his invasion of three Muslim nations. Yet, his strategy to force seven more nations to support a covenant with Israel seemed reckless. Isaiah calls it a covenant with death.

'After these things I looked, and behold, a door standing open in heaven. And the first voice which I heard was like a trumpet speaking with me, saying, "Come up here, and I will show you things which must take place after this." Revelation 4:1

Many Christians believe John going up to heaven represents the resurrection of believers. When a voice like a trumpet speaks, they insist the church will enter a door into heaven. **(Rev. 4:1)** Saints, nowhere does it say John is symbolic of the body of Christ. There is no resurrection in this passage. John is going up in the Spirit to witness the events that shall take place before, during, and after the Second Coming of Christ. **(Rev. 1:19)**

'And I saw in the right hand of Him who sat on the throne a scroll written inside and on the back, sealed with seven seals.' Revelation 5:1

After the Little Horn physically subdues three Muslim nations, the saints watching will know the 70th week is near. **(Dan. 7:7-8, 20-25)** The next event takes place in heaven. **(Rev. 5:1)** God Almighty is sitting on His throne. He is holding a heavenly scroll. There is writing on the inside and on the back. It is sealed with seven seals. No one in heaven or earth can open the scroll. **(Rev. 5:3)**

'Then I saw a strong angel proclaiming with a loud voice, "Who is worthy to open the scroll and to loose its seals." Revelation 5:2

In his vision, John saw a strong angel asking who is worthy to open the heavenly scroll? An elder announces only the Lion from the tribe of Judah, the Lamb of God, can open the scroll and loose its seals. **(Rev. 5:2-5; 6:1-17; 8:1)**

'Again, the next day, John stood with two of his disciples. And looking at Jesus as He walked, he said, "Behold the Lamb of God." John 1:35-36

John the Baptist called Jesus the Lamb of God who takes away the sin of the world. In the midst of the throne stood the Lamb. **(Rev. 5:6)** Only the blood of the slain Lamb has the power to redeem believers. **(John 1:35-36)**

'Then He came and took the scroll out of the right hand of Him who sat on the throne. Now when He had taken the scroll, the four living creatures and the twenty-four elders fell down before the Lamb, each having a harp, and golden bowls full of incense, which are the prayers of the saints.' Revelation 5:7-8

The Lamb will take the scroll from the right hand of God Almighty. In adoration, the four living creatures and the twenty-four elders will fall down before the Lamb. They're holding golden bowls full of incense; which are the prayers of the saints. **(Rev. 5:7-8)**

'Now I saw when the Lamb opened one of the seals; and I heard one of the four living creatures saying with a voice like thunder, "Come and see." And I looked, and behold, a white horse. He who sat on it had a bow; and a crown was given to him, and he went out conquering and to conquer.' Revelation 6:1-2

"...Take heed that you not be deceived. For many will come in My name, saying, 'I am He,' and, 'The time has drawn near.' Therefore, do not go after them." Luke 21:8

"So you also, when you see all these things, know that it is near—at the doors!" Matthew 24:33

"Remember therefore how you have received and heard; hold fast and repent. Therefore if you will not watch, I will come upon you as a thief, and you will not know what hour I will come upon you." Revelation 3:3

A white horse will appear after the Lamb opens the first seal. Its rider is holding a bow. He is given a crown. We aren't told who this rider is. His mission is to conquer many believers. (Rev. 6:1-2) This is why our Lord is warning us to watch and not to be deceived. (Mat. 24:4-5) What is this great deception and when will it take place? At the beginning of the 70th week of Daniel, after the opening of the first seal, many Christians won't be watching for the events Jesus shared while on the Mount of Olives. (Mat. 24:3-31, Rev. 6:1-7) Instead, they'll be deceived by false teachers insisting His coming must come first; at any moment. (Luke 21:8) In other words, they'll be blindsided by not watching for the events warning us the Coming of the Son of Man is near-at the doors. (Mat. 24:33) Anyone refusing to watch will not know the hour of His coming. (Rev. 3:3)

4. He Will Confirm A Covenant

> A host of angels, the four living creatures, and the twenty-four elders watched as the Lamb of God opened the first seal of the heavenly scroll. A rider on a beautiful white horse instantly appears. His mission is to conquer many souls on earth.

'Then he shall confirm a covenant with many for one week...' Daniel 9:27a

Why a covenant between Israel and her enemies? Every night the war between Israel and Islam is seen on news channels all over the world. The nations can only watch as the killing drags on. Children on both sides are being traumatized. The buildup of hate is so fierce a truce seems impossible. It's clear, only an outsider will be capable of negotiating an end to this violence. The prophecies of Daniel and Revelation highlight this covenant between Israel and her surrounding enemies. The stage is being set for the 70th week of Daniel to begin. **(Dan. 9:24, 27a)**

'And another sign appeared in heaven: behold, a great, fiery red dragon having seven heads and ten horns, and seven diadems on his heads.' Revelation 12:3

As we studied earlier, John saw both the Dragon and the Beast having ten horns and seven heads. The ten horns represent the ten nations that will give their power to the Beast. **(Rev. 17:12-13)** The seven heads represent the seven leaders that failed to destroy the children of Israel. **(Rev. 12:3; 13:1)**

'There are also seven kings. Five have fallen, one is, and the other has not yet come. And when he comes, he must continue a short time.' Revelation 17:10

1. Pharaoh of Egypt in 1450 B.C.

2. Shalmaneser V of Assyria in 722 B.C.

3. Nebuchadnezzar of Babylon in 586 B.C.

4. Xerxes of Medo-Persia in 536 B.C.

5. Antiochus Epiphanes of Greece in 175 B.C.

6. Domitian of Rome in 96 A.D.

When John wrote his letter in the first century, Domitian of Rome was the sixth head. So, who was the seventh head who came for a short time (1939-1945), yet killed more Jews than the previous six heads combined? That's right, the seventh head was Adolph Hitler of Nazi Germany. **(Rev. 17:10)**

'The beast...is himself also the eighth, and is of the seven, and is going to perdition.' Revelation 17:11

The future eighth head, the Beast, will come from the previous seven heads. **(Rev. 17:11)** He may be the future leader of one of these seven nations. Or his nationality may be Egyptian, Assyrian, Iraqi, Iranian, Greek, Italian, or German. Trying to figure out the identity of the Man of Sin (Beast) before he is revealed on the world stage has deceived so many. **(2 Thes. 2:3-4)** With famous prophecy teachers making non-stop false predictions, this only feeds into the mounting hysteria. Let's remember, patience will play a key role for those getting the victory over the Beast. **(Rev. 13:10; 14:12; 15:2)** This is why our Lord is exhorting us to watch! **(Rev. 3:3; 16:15)**

"The ten horns which you saw are ten kings who have received no kingdom as yet, but they receive authority for one hour as kings with the beast. These are of one mind, and they will give their power and authority to the beast." Revelation 17:12-13

The 70th week of Daniel will begin when Israel and the ten nations (horns) supporting the Beast agree to seven-year covenant of peace. **(Rev. 17:12-13, Dan. 9:27a)** These ten horns may include Jordan, Egypt, Saudi Arabia, Iran, Syria, Lebanon, Turkey, Libya, Ethiopia and Iraq. In the first half of the 70th week, the Jewish people and her Muslim enemies will be living in peace. **(Ezek. 38:1-14, Psa. 83)**

'And I looked, and behold, a white horse. He who sat on it had a bow; and a crown was given to him, and he went out conquering and to conquer.' Revelation 6:2

The 70th week will be confirmed by the Beast the same day the Lamb of God opens the first seal of the heavenly scroll. **(Rev. 6:1-2)** These two events will initiate the seven-year week which will include the Beginning of Sorrows **(Mat. 24:8)**, the Great Tribulation **(Mat. 24:9-26)** and some the events of the Day of the Lord. **(Mat. 24:37-39, Rev. 8:13; 9:1-21)**

'So they worshiped the dragon who gave authority to the beast; and they worshiped the beast, saying, "Who is like the beast? Who is able to make war with him?" Revelation 13:4

The nations will rejoice over the Beast, the eighth head, for bringing peace to the Middle East. World leaders will honor this leader for ending the age-old conflict between Jews and Muslims. What they don't know is their new hero is going to break this covenant by invading an unsuspecting Jerusalem in exactly forty-two months. **(Mat. 24:15, Luke 21:20, Rev. 13:3-5)**

"Through his cunning He shall cause deceit to prosper under his rule; And he shall exalt himself in his heart. He shall destroy many in their prosperity. He shall even rise against the Prince of princes; But he shall be broken without human means." Daniel 8:25

Those obeying the Holy Spirit will be watching when the seven-year covenant between Israel and her enemies is confirmed. **(Dan. 9:27a)** They will know the 70th week of Daniel has begun. They will also know the nationality of the Beast (Antichrist), the country he is from, and the ten Muslim nations (horns) supporting his evil agenda. **(Rev.17:12-13)** May we never underestimate the spiritual warfare we will experience after this covenant is confirmed. **(Dan. 8:25)** Exposing the Beast when the world is declaring him a miracle worker won't be easy. **(Rev. 13:4)**

5. The Temple Of God

> Jews and Muslims flooded the streets in celebration. In a sign of unity, the Israeli Prime Minster and the leaders of ten Muslim nations joined hands. The nations are calling this peace covenant a miracle from God. The saints watching understood.

'Then I was given a reed like a measuring rod. And the angel stood, saying, "Rise and measure the temple of God, the altar, and those who worship there." Revelation 11:1

The cry of the Jewish people to build their temple atop Mount Moriah is at fever pitch. The Sanhedrin has miraculously been reinstated. The sacred instruments for worship are on display. The priests are prepared to perform animal sacrifices. This is the temple highlighted by Jesus, Daniel, Paul, and John. **(Mat. 24:15, Dan. 9:27, 2 Thes. 2:4, Rev. 11:2)** This tabernacle of David may be similar to the tabernacle used in the wilderness for forty years. **(Acts 15:15-17, Deut. 8:2, Exod. 28:43; 29:30)**

'But leave out the court which is outside the temple, and do not measure it, for it has been given to the Gentiles. And they will tread the holy city underfoot for forty-two months.' Revelation 11:2

Why will Israel's enemies allow this Temple to be built during the 70th week of Daniel? There are twenty-one dictatorships surrounding Israel believing the Jewish people are evil and must be destroyed. According to the purpose of God, the Muslims will allow Israeli priests to build their temple in Jerusalem. **(Rev. 17:17)** It will rest beside the El Aksa Mosque; the third holiest site in Islam. **(Rev. 11:2)**

'And forces shall be mustered by him, and they shall defile the sanctuary fortress; then they shall take away the daily sacrifices, and place there the abomination of desolation.' Daniel 11:31

"Therefore, when you see the 'abomination of desolation,' spoken of by Daniel the prophet, standing in the holy place," (whoever reads, let him understand).' Matthew 24:15

Who will stand in the Holy Place? The abomination of desolation is a Hebrew expression for worshiping an idol in the place of God. In the middle of the 70th week, the abomination that causes desolation will take away the daily sacrifices the priests of Judaism have reinstituted. Why do demons attack when this is studied? Jesus wants every believer to understand the identity of the Abomination of Desolation and his evil agenda for the world. **(Dan. 9:27; 11:31, Mark 13:14-19, Mat. 24:15)**

'...But in the middle of the week He shall bring an end to sacrifice and offering. And on the wing of abominations shall be one who makes desolate...' Daniel 9:27

When will this future temple of God be built? In the first half of the 70th week, the Beast will muster an army from His ten horns. **(Dan. 7:24; 11:31-32, Rev. 17:12-13)** These Muslim forces are going to obey him in the assault of an unsuspecting Jerusalem. **(Ezek. 38:11-14, Luke 21:20)** The Abomination of Desolation (Beast) and his armies will defile the holy place in the middle of the 70th week. Which means the temple of God will be built sometime in the first half of this seven-year week. **(Dan. 9:27, Mat. 24:15, 2 Thes. 2:3-4)**

6. Second Seal: The Red Horse

> Atop Mount Moriah, Jewish workers are rebuilding their Temple. Priests are preparing to give daily sacrifices. Everyone is praising the world leader who made it possible. FOX, CNN, Facebook, Twitter, his face is everywhere.

'When He opened the second seal, I heard the second living creature saying, "Come and see." Another horse, fiery red, went out. And it was granted to the one who sat on it to take peace from the earth, and that people should kill one another...' Revelation 6:3-4

Sometime in the first half of the 70th week, the Lamb will open the second seal of the heavenly scroll. A rider on a fiery red horse will appear. We aren't told his name. He is coming to take peace from the earth. He will achieve this by having people kill each other. We aren't told how many will die. (Rev. 6:3-4)

"And you will hear of wars and rumors of wars. See that you are not troubled; for all these things must come to pass, but the end is not yet." Matthew 24:6

After the first seal opens, false teachers will begin deceiving many believers. (Rev. 6:1-2, Mat. 24:4-5, Luke 21:8) Wars will spread among the nations after the second seal is opened. (Rev. 6:3-4, Mat. 24:6) Jesus exhorts us not to be troubled because the end of the age is not yet (harvest). The harvest of believers will take place after the Lamb of God opens the sixth seal of the heavenly scroll. (Mat. 13:39-43; 24:29-31, Rev. 6:12-17)

"For nation will rise against nation..." Matthew 24:7a

How will Christians recognize the wars from the second seal? The Lamb of God will open the seven seals of the heavenly scroll within the 70th week. **(Rev. 8:1)** The killing between the nations after the opening of the second seal will take place in the first half of the seven years. **(Mat. 24:6-7a, Rev. 6:3-4)** Which means the wars from our past, even the wars we are seeing today, have nothing to do with the future 70th week. **(Dan. 9:27, Mat. 24:15)**

"I will go up against a land of unwalled villages; I will go to a peaceful people, who dwell safely, all of them dwelling without walls, and having neither bars nor gates." Ezekiel 38:11

The Jewish people will be living peacefully in the first half of the 70th week. We know this because Jerusalem will be unprotected when the Abomination of Desolation and his armies invade her in the middle of the seven-year week. **(Dan. 9:27, Mat. 24:15, Ezek. 38:11, 14, Luke 21:20)**

"...The harvest is the end of the age, and the reapers are the angels...But he who endures to the end shall be saved." Matthew 13:39; 24:13

The harvest is the gathering of believers by angels at the coming of the Son of Man. The great multitude of overcomers getting the victory over the Beast will be delivered from the wrath to come. **(Rev. 7:9-17; 15:2, 1 Thes. 1:10)** This is why we should not be troubled when we see the spread of wars in the first half of the 70th week. **(Mat. 24:6, Rev. 6:3-4)** Instead, we should be anticipating our physical redemption after the sun, moon, and stars lose their light! **(Mat. 24:29, Luke 21:28, Rev. 6:12-17, Isa. 13:9-11, Joel 2:30-31)**

7. The Great Harlot

> The second seal is open. A rider on a fiery red horse is taking peace from the earth. The rumors of wars came first. No one really knew when the carnage started. The savage killing between the nations is unimaginable.

"Come, I will show you the judgment of the great harlot who sits on many waters, with whom the kings of the earth committed fornication, and the inhabitants of the earth were made drunk with the wine of her fornication." Revelation 17:1-2

Since her inception, the Great Harlot sitting on many waters has beguiled the world leaders of earth. This has led many to drink the wine of her fornication. Those corrupted by this evil counterfeit would never think they're being deceived. **(Rev. 17:1-2; 14:8; 19:2)**

'So he carried me away in the Spirit into the wilderness. And I saw a woman sitting on a scarlet beast which was full of names of blasphemy, having seven heads and ten horns.' Revelation 17:3

'Then I stood on the sand of the sea. And I saw a beast rising up out of the sea, having seven heads and ten horns, and on his horns ten crowns, and on his heads a blasphemous name.' Revelation 13:1

An angel carries the apostle into the wilderness. John saw a woman sitting on a scarlet beast full of names of blasphemy. She is called the mother of harlots. The beast has seven heads and ten horns. As we previously studied, this beast represents Satan's world system in these last days. **(Rev. 17:3; 13:1)**

'The woman was arrayed in purple and scarlet, and adorned with gold and precious stones and pearls, having in her hand a golden cup full of abominations and the filthiness of her fornication.' Revelation 17:4

The harlot is arrayed in purple and scarlet. The gold and pearls she is wearing represent her vast wealth. She is holding a golden cup full of the filthiness of her fornication. Written on her forehead is Mystery Babylon the Great! **(Rev.17:4-5; 18:3; 19:2)**

'I saw the woman, drunk with the blood of the saints and with the blood of the martyrs of Jesus. And when I saw her, I marveled with great amazement' Revelation 17:6

The woman is drunk with the blood of the saints and martyrs of Jesus. The seven mountains she is sitting on is the city of Rome. She is riding Satan's beast system that has come back to life. **(Rev. 17:6-9; 19:2; 13:3)**

"...We will surely keep our vows that we have made, to burn incense to the queen of heaven and pour out drink offerings to her..." Jeremiah 44:25

Satan created the first pagan religion on earth. Babylon was ruled by King Nimrod and Queen Semiramis. Jeremiah warned the children of Israel not to make vows to the queen of heaven, Semiramis. Today, millions are making daily vows to their queen of heaven. They believe Mary is sitting at the right hand of God. Such blasphemy is from the lips of Satan. **(Jer. 44:16-25, Heb. 10:12)**

"Do not call anyone on earth your father; for One is your Father, He who is in heaven." Matthew 23:9

Over one billion Catholics believe the pope has primacy over the world. In submission, they call him their most Holy Father. They believe anyone refusing to trust in the Vicar of Christ is cursed of God. Why is this a doctrine of demons? There is only one Holy Father and He is in heaven. **(Mat. 23:9, John 17:11)**

'For there is one God and one Mediator between God and men, the Man Christ Jesus.' 1 Timothy 2:5

"But that you may know that the Son of Man has power on earth to forgive sins..." Mark 2:10

To be Catholic, one must believe Mary is co-redeemer with Jesus. What is the fate of those believing in this evil heresy? Christ Jesus is the mediator between God and man. **(1 Tim. 2:5)** Anyone rejecting this truth is rejecting the Son of God; the only One having the power to forgive sins. **(Mark 2:10, Acts 4:12)**

'And in her was found the blood of prophets and saints, and of all who were slain on the earth.' Revelation 18:24

The pope teaches all faiths are praying to the same God. This is why so many religious leaders are traveling to Rome to pray for world peace. The agenda of this ecumenical cult is to become one family. Their evil mantra is all people are His children. The harlot has already begun the reconciliation of all religions. Yet, the most influential Christian leaders in the world remain silent. In the end, the blood of the prophets and the saints will be found in her (all false religions). **(Rev. 18:24; 17:5)**

"Take heed that no one deceives you. For many will come in My name, saying, 'I am the Christ,' and will deceive many." Matthew 24:4-5

Who is falsely coming in His name? A respected Catholic priest was once asked, "If one does not believe in Jesus will they go to hell?" This theologian quickly replied they won't. He assured his audience it's not God's job to cast people into hell. This wolf is coming in Christ's name while denying the gospel. Our Lord is warning believers not to be deceived by such trickery. Sadly, many already are. **(Mat. 24:4-5, Acts 20:29)**

'Thus he shall act against the strongest fortresses with a foreign god, which he shall acknowledge, and advance its glory; and he shall cause them to rule over many, and divide the land for gain.' Daniel 11:39

While the riders of the white, red, and black horses are razing havoc during the first half of the seven-year week, the Beast will advance the glory of a foreign god. **(Rev. 6:1-6, Dan. 11:39)** In return, the mother of harlots will support this deceiver in his takeover of the nations. Once the Beast gains control the nations in the middle of the seven-year week, this evil religious system will no longer be needed. The ten horns of the Beast will hate the harlot and make her desolate. **(Rev. 13:3-7; 17:16)**

8. Third Seal: The Black Horse

> Under the guise of Mystery Babylon, all faiths are seeking after unity. With the death toll rising, the Harlot agrees to support the Beast in his takeover of the nations. This coup will take place when his ten horns invade an unsuspecting Jerusalem.

"For nation will rise against nation, and kingdom against kingdom. And there will be famines, pestilences, and earthquakes in various places. All these are the beginning of sorrows." Matthew 24:4-8

While on the Mount of Olives, Jesus shared the events that will take place in the first half of the 70th week. He calls them the Beginning of Sorrows. John saw these same events. (Rev. 6:1-6)

First seal- False teachers will deceive many believers.
(Mat. 24:4-5, Rev. 6:1-2)

Second seal- Wars will spread among the nations.
(Mat. 24:6, Rev. 6:3-4)

Third seal- Famines, pestilences, and earthquakes will erupt.
(Mat. 24:7, Rev. 6:5-6)

'When He opened the third seal, I heard the third living creature say, "Come and see." So I looked, and behold, a black horse, and he who sat on it had a pair of scales in his hand." Revelation 6:6

After the Lamb opens the third seal, a rider on a black horse will come down having a pair of scales. A daily wage won't be able to buy much food as famines, pestilences, and earthquakes devastate the earth. **(Rev. 6:5-6, Mat. 24:7)**

"Therefore when you see the 'abomination of desolation,' spoken of by Daniel the prophet, standing in the holy place" (whoever reads, let him understand).' Matthew 24:15

When will the Beginning of Sorrows begin and end? **(Mat. 24:4-8, Rev. 6:1-6)** The 70th week of Daniel will be confirmed the day the Lamb opens the first seal. Forty-two months later, in the middle of the week, the famines, pestilences, and earthquakes from the third seal will cease. The opening of the fourth seal **(Rev. 6:7-8)**, the Abomination of Desolation standing in the holy place, will initiate the Great Tribulation of the saints! **(Mat. 24:15-22, Rev. 13:5)**

'For when they say, "Peace and safety!" then sudden destruction comes upon them, as labor pains upon a pregnant woman. And they shall not escape.'
1 Thessalonians 5:3

When will the wicked be declaring peace and safety during the 70th week of Daniel? **(1 Thes. 5:3)** Will it be during the Beginning of Sorrows, the Great Tribulation or the Day of the Lord?

During the Beginning of Sorrows, the wicked won't be declaring peace and safety while being devastated by the wars, famines, pestilences and earthquakes. **(Mat. 24:4-8)**

During the Day of the Lord, the wicked won't be declaring peace and safety while God punishes them for their evil. **(Mat. 24:37-39, Isa. 13:9-11)**

The nations will feel safe after the wars, famines, pestilences, and earthquakes disappear. **(Mat. 24:4-8)** The only time the wicked will be declaring peace and safety will be during the Great Tribulation of the saints by the Beast. **(Mat. 24:9-26, 1 Thes. 5:3, Rev. 13:5-7)**

9. The Woman Having Twelve Stars

> The third seal is open. A rider on a black horse appears holding a pair of scales. Almost overnight massive food shortages turned into catastrophic famines. Coupled with lethal pestilences and earthquakes, the wicked had no idea why this is happening.

'Now a great sign appeared in heaven: a woman clothed with the sun, with the moon under her feet, and on her head a garland of twelve stars.' Revelation 12:1

The woman clothed in the sun is a picture of Israel. (Rev. 12:1-6) The twelve stars on her head represent 144,000 men from the twelve tribes of Israel. They will be redeemed by God after the resurrection of the elect. (Rev. 7:1-8, 9-17; 14:1-4)

'And He said to them, "I saw Satan fall like lightning from heaven." Luke 10:18

Because of his rebellion against God, Satan fell like lightening from heaven. This judgment took place before mankind was created. It was the serpent who deceived Adam and Eve into sinning against God. Because of their disobedience, they were expelled out of the garden into a world of spiritual darkness ruled by Satan. (Luke 10:18, Gen. 3:1-24, John 14:30)

'Then being with child, she cried out in labor and in pain to give birth...And the dragon stood before the woman who was ready to give birth, to devour her Child as soon as it was born. She bore a male Child who was to rule all nations with a rod of iron. And her Child was caught up to God and His throne.' Revelation 12:2, 4-5

Satan was prepared to devour the Christ child as soon as He was born. It never happened. On the third day, the Father raised His Son from the dead and caught Him up to His throne. Jesus will soon rule all the nations with a rod of iron for a thousand years. **(Rev. 12:4-5, Mark 9:31, Rev. 20:6)**

'Then the woman fled into the wilderness, where she has a place prepared by God, that they should feed her there one thousand two hundred and sixty days.' Revelation 12:6

The focus of John's vision now shifts to the future 70th Week of Daniel. A calendar year in Daniel's day was 360 days. This seven-year week is divided into two halves of 1,260 days. **(Rev. 12:6, Dan. 9:27, Mat. 24:15)** When you read one thousand two hundred and sixty days, a time and times and half a time (3 ½ years), or forty-two months, it's always referring to the second half of the seven-year week. **(Rev. 11:3; 12:14; 13:5, Dan. 12:7)**

In the middle of the seven-year week, Satan will attempt to persecute the woman who gave birth to the Christ child. This is why a remnant living in Israel will flee to a place in the wilderness prepared by God. She will be protected for the entire second half of the seven-year week. **(Rev. 12:6-14, Zech. 13:8-9)**

10. The Restrainer

> Since signing the covenant, Israel is living in complete safety. With multiple wars ripping nation's apart, Jewish leaders are convinced God is protecting them. This is why the exodus of millions fleeing into the wilderness seemed so mysterious.

'For the mystery of lawlessness is already at work; only He who now restrains will do so until He is taken out of the way.' 2 Thessalonians 2:7

'And he was given a mouth speaking great things and blasphemies, and he was given authority to continue for forty-two months.' Revelation 13:5

During the Beginning of Sorrows, the first half of the seven-year week, the Restrainer will prevent the Mystery of Lawlessness from attacking Israel. After he is taken out of the way, Satan will give his authority over the nations to the Beast for forty-two months. **(Mat. 24:4-8, 2 Thes. 2:7, Dan. 12:1, Rev. 13:2-7)**

"Anyone who speaks a word against the Son of Man, it will be forgiven him; but whoever speaks against the Holy Spirit, it will not be forgiven him, either in this age or in the age to come." Matthew 12:32

Who is the restrainer? Paul calls the restrainer a he. **(2 Thes. 2:7)** The church is a she, so the body of Christ isn't the restrainer. The Holy Spirit isn't either. Why not? There will be people receiving the Holy Spirit during the Great Tribulation, during the Day of the Lord, and even during the 1,000-year reign of Christ. **(Rev. 12:17; 14:4; 21:24)** The Holy Spirit will never be taken away in this age; nor in the age to come, the reign of Christ over the nations. **(Mat. 12:32, Rev. 20:6)**

"But I will tell you what is noted in the Scripture of Truth. (No one upholds me against these, except Michael your prince." Daniel 10:21

Michael, the great prince, is presently watching over the sons of Israel. **(Dan. 10:21)** During the Beginning of Sorrows, this angel will be restraining the mystery of lawlessness from attacking Jerusalem. **(Mat. 24:4-8, 2 Thes. 2:7)**

'At that time Michael shall stand up, the great prince who stands watch over the sons of your people; and there shall be a time of trouble, such as never was since there was a nation...' Daniel 12:1a

In the middle of the seven-year week, Michael will stand up (stop restraining). **(Dan. 12:1)** This event will initiate the Great Tribulation; a time of trouble believers have never experienced. **(Dan. 12:1, Mat. 24:15-22)** An unsuspecting Israel will be totally caught off guard. **(Ezek. 38:11)** Once Michael the restrainer is taken out of the way **(2 Thes. 2:7)** the Abomination of Desolation and his armies from ten Muslim nations (horns) will begin their wrath by invading an unsuspecting Jerusalem. **(Mat. 24:15, Rev. 17:10-11, Luke 21:20)**

11. A War In Heaven

> Israel was faithfully protected during the Beginning of Sorrows. Standing up, Michael withdrew his restraint over the mystery of lawlessness. Satan instantly summoned his angels to war. A time of trouble is coming the church has never experienced.

'Now there was a day when the sons of God came to present themselves before the Lord, and Satan also came among them. And the Lord said to Satan, "From where do you come?" So Satan answered the Lord and said, "From going to and from on the earth, and from walking back and forth on it." Job 1:6-7

Satan was once a beautiful Cherub; having an anointed ministry in heaven. His ways were perfect until iniquity was found in him. His wisdom corrupted, he was cast to earth. **(Ezek. 28:14-17, Luke 10:18)** Even though he lost his exalted position in heaven; Satan was still able to accuse Job while in the presence of the Lord. **(Job 1:6-12)** He also asked God to sift Peter like wheat. **(Luke 22:31)** The Devil is currently roaming the earth as a devouring lion while accusing believers before God day and night. **(1 Pet. 5:8, Rev. 12:10)**

'Then the woman fled into the wilderness, where she has a place prepared by God, that they should feed her there one thousand two hundred and sixty days. 'And war broke out in heaven: Michael and his angels fought with the dragon; and the dragon and his angels fought.' Revelation 12:6-7

A remnant from Israel (woman) will flee into the wilderness by the middle of the 70th week (1,260 days). Once she reaches a place prepared by God, a war will break out in heaven. Michael and his angels will fight against the Dragon and his angels. **(Rev. 12:6-7)**

'But they did not prevail, nor was a place found for them in heaven any longer. So the great dragon was cast out, that serpent of old, called the Devil and Satan, who deceives the whole world; he was cast to the earth, and his angels were cast out with him.' Revelation 12:8-9

The war between angels of light and angels of darkness is over. The Dragon did not prevail. The Devil who is deceiving the whole world will no longer find a place in heaven. **(Rev. 12:8-9)**

'Then I heard a loud voice saying in heaven, "Now salvation, and strength, and the kingdom of our God, and the power of His Christ have come, for the accuser of our brethren, who accused them before our God day and night, has been cast down."' Revelation 12:10

A loud voice will announce the accuser of the brethren has been cast down by the power of Christ. Everyone in heaven will be rejoicing. They'll never see his hideous face again. It will be a different story for the inhabitants of earth. **(Rev. 12:10-12)**

'Now when the dragon saw that he had been cast to the earth, he persecuted the woman who gave birth to the male Child...And the dragon was enraged with the woman, and he went to make war with the rest of her offspring, who keep the commandments of God and have the testimony of Jesus Christ.' Revelation 12:13, 17

Michael will cast the Dragon down to earth in the middle of the 70th week. **(Rev. 12:6-12; 13:3-5)** The Devil will begin by trying to persecute the woman. He will become furious because this remnant from Israel is being protected in the wilderness. The Devil will turn away and make war against those having the testimony of Jesus Christ. **(Rev. 12:13-17, Mat. 24:21-22)**

'...For the Devil has come down to you, having great wrath, because he knows that he has a short time.' Revelation 12:12

"For then there will be great tribulation, such as has not been since the beginning of the world until this time, no, nor ever shall be. And unless those days were shortened, no flesh would be saved; but for the elect's sake those days will be shortened" Matthew 24:21-22.

The Devil is coming down with great wrath because his time to deceive is short. **(Rev. 12:6-12)** He doesn't have to be told when his wrath against the saints will end. The days of the Great Tribulation will be shortened when the Son of Man sends forth His angels to gather overcomers from every nation. **(Mat. 24:21-22, 29-31, Rev. 7:9-17)**

12. The Beast

> By the power of Christ, Michael the restrainer cast the accuser of the brethren out of heaven for the final time. The Devil is coming with great wrath because his time to deceive is short. He knows when overcomers will look up for their redemption.

'...The dragon gave him his power, his throne, and great authority...And all the world marveled and followed the beast.' Revelation 13:2-3

In 96 A.D., John wrote down The Revelation of Jesus Christ. **(Rev. 1:1-3)** When this letter was read to the churches, Satan understood his demise. He heard when believers will be delivered from his wrath. **(Rev. 7:9-17)** He heard when he will lose control of this world. **(Rev. 11:15)** He even heard when he will be cast into the lake of fire. **(Rev. 20:10)** In a futile attempt to prevent this Satan has devised a plan. He is going to grant his power and his throne to a man. John calls him the Beast. **(Rev. 13:2-3)**

'And he was given a mouth speaking great things and blasphemies, and he was given authority to continue for forty-two months. Then he opened his mouth in blasphemy against God, to blaspheme His name, His tabernacle, and those who dwell in heaven.' Revelation 13:5-6

Satan will give the Beast his authority over the nations for forty-two months; the second half of the seven-year week. The world will marvel and follow their new leader. So much so, they will worship him and the Dragon. **(Rev. 13:3-6)**

'You will say, 'I will go up against a land of unwalled villages; I will go to a peaceful people, who dwell safely, all of them dwelling without walls, and having neither bars nor gates.' Ezekiel 38:11

In the middle of the seven-year week, the Beast and his armies will break the covenant he confirmed with Israel by invading an unsuspecting Jerusalem. **(Mat. 24:15, Luke 21:20)** The leaders of ten nations giving their authority to the Beast will come from the Middle East. Ezekiel saw this vicious invasion by surrounding nations in a vision. **(Ezek. 38:11)** The nations supporting the Beast may include Jordan, Egypt, Saudi Arabia, Iran, Syria, Lebanon, Turkey, Libya, Ethiopia and Iraq. **(Rev. 17:12-13)**

'And he shall plant the tents of his palace between the seas and the glorious holy mountain...' Daniel 11:45

Where will the Beast rule from during the 70th week? After invading Jerusalem, the Antichrist will rule from the glorious holy mountain, the Temple Mount. **(Dan. 11:45)**

'So they worshiped the dragon who gave authority to the beast; and they worshiped the beast, saying, "Who is like the beast? Who is able to make war with him? And he was given a mouth speaking great things and blasphemies, and he was given authority to continue for forty-two months.' Revelation 13:4-5

Depending on the context, the Beast can be the man the world will worship or his kingdom. **(Rev. 13:4-5; 16:10)** Everyone must choose who to follow. **(Rev. 14:9-11)** This is why discerning those no longer serving God will be so critical. **(Mal. 3:18, Luke 21:16)**

"I was watching; and the same horn was making war against the saints and prevailing against them.' Daniel 7:21

Most believe their favorite teacher is being led by the Holy Spirit. We often hear, my pastor taught it, I believe it, that settles it. In other words, he can't be wrong. How is Satan using such blind allegiance to deceive? On any given Sunday, smiling pastors all over the world are teaching, "The Antichrist will never prevail over the saints. Don't be concerned, it's not even a salvation issue." Tragically, many professing Christ are trusting in this dangerous Trojan Horse message coming from deceiving spirits. **(Dan. 7:21)**

'It was granted to him to make war with the saints and to overcome them. And authority was given him over every tribe, tongue, and nation.' Revelation 13:7

How will the Beast war against the saints? He will begin by speaking blasphemy against God, His name, His tabernacle and those dwelling in heaven. **(Rev. 13:6, 2 Thes. 2:3-4)** The nations will worship the Beast during the Great Tribulation. **(Mat. 24:21-22, Rev. 13:1-18; 14:9-11)** The saints not willing to be persecuted or martyred will be in great danger. **(Mat. 24:9-10, Rev. 13:7)**

'And then the lawless one will be revealed, whom the Lord will consume with the breath of His mouth and destroy with the brightness of His coming.' 2 Thessalonians 2:8

It's important to understand when the Man of Sin is revealed, when the Lawless One is stripped of his power and when the Beast is consumed.

The Man of Sin will be revealed in the middle of the 70th week.
(2 Thes. 2:3-8, Mat. 24:15)

The Lawless One will be paralyzed by the Son of Man.
(2 Thes. 2:8, Mat. 24:37-39)

The Beast will be consumed by the Word of God.
(2 Thes. 2:8, Rev. 19:11-21)

13. The False Prophet

> After the Beast confirmed the false peace with Israel, the overcomers understood. Convincing members from their church, their friends, even their own family, was another story. The invasion of Jerusalem is near. The brainwashing is horrific.

'Another beast coming up out of the earth, and he had two horns like a lamb and spoke like a dragon.' Revelation 13:11

In the middle of the 70th week, what religious leader will look like a lamb yet speak like a dragon? **(Rev. 13:11)** John calls him the False Prophet. **(Rev. 16:13)** This seemingly good man is actually an evil counterfeit. John describes this unholy trinity. **(Rev. 20:10)**

The Dragon is Satan. **(Rev. 12:9)**
The Beast is the first beast. **(Rev. 13:2-7)**
The False Prophet is the second beast. **(Rev. 13:11-18)**

'And he exercises all the authority of the first beast in his presence, and causes the earth and those who dwell in it to worship the first beast...' Revelation 13:12

During the Great Tribulation, the False Prophet will exercise all the authority of the Beast while in his presence. He will cause those dwelling on the earth to worship the Beast and receive his mark. **(Mat. 24:21-22, Rev. 13:12-18; 14:9-10)**

'He performs great signs, so that he even makes fire come down from heaven on the earth in the sight of men. And he deceives those who dwell on the earth by those signs which he was granted to do in the sight of the beast...' Revelation 13:13-14a

Satan will grant the False Prophet the power to perform great signs. This evil imposter will deceive the world by calling fire down from heaven. **(Rev 13:13-14a)**

'He was granted power to give breath to the image of the beast, that the image of the beast should both speak and cause as many as would not worship the image of the beast to be killed.' Revelation 13:15

Who will be killed during Satan's wrath? **(Rev 12:12)** During the days of the Great Tribulation **(Rev. 6:7-11)**, the False Prophet will have the power to force the world to worship the image of the Beast. **(Rev. 13:15)** Any saint caught, refusing to obey, will be killed. **(Rev. 20:4)**

'He causes all...to receive a mark on their right hand or on their foreheads, and that no one may buy or sell except one who has the mark or the name of the beast, or the number of his name.' Revelation 13:16-17

During the second half of the seven-year week, anyone not having the mark of the Beast will not be able to buy or sell anything. John doesn't tell us how long it will take the False Prophet to complete this deception. The saints refusing to cooperate won't be called loving Christians. We may be labeled religious fanatics, racists, even terrorists. **(Rev. 13:16-18; 14:9-11)**

'Many shall be purified, made white, and refined, but...none of the wicked shall understand, but the wise shall understand.' Daniel 12:10

"Behold, am coming quickly! Hold fast what you have, that no one may take your crown." Revelation 3:11

During the Great Tribulation of the saints, the wise will understand. **(Dan. 12:10)** There is no way of knowing how many will choose martyrdom rather than deny their Lord. **(Rev. 20:4a)** Jesus is warning us to hold fast till He comes back. **(Rev. 3:11)** Allowing the Beasts to take our crown is not an option. **(Rev. 13:7-10)**

14. Fourth Seal: The Pale Horse

> During the hideous famines and pestilences, the love of one man stood out. His shipments of food and medicine saved many lives. His bringing of faiths together is a miracle. For many, he can do no wrong. The saints call him the False Prophet.

'When He opened the fourth seal, I heard the voice of the fourth living creature saying, 'Come and see.' So I looked, and behold, a pale horse...the name of him who sat on it was Death, and Hades followed with him...' Revelation 6:7-8

During the Beginning of Sorrows, we won't know the names of the riders of the white, red, or black horses. **(Mat. 24:4-8, Rev. 6:1-6)** A pale horse will appear after the opening of the fourth seal. Its rider is called Death. And Hades is following after him. **(Rev. 6:7-8)**

'...And power was given to them over a fourth of the earth, to kill with sword, with hunger, with death, and by the beasts of the earth.' Revelation 6:8b

Death and Hades will have the power to kill over a fourth of the earth during the Great Tribulation of the saints. **(Mat. 24:21-22, Dan. 12:1)** They will kill by the two beasts. **(Rev. 6:8b)** 'Beast' is used thirty-two times in The Revelation of Jesus Christ. The world will worship the first Beast having seven heads and ten horns. **(Rev. 13:1-10)** The False Prophet, the second beast, will cause those on earth to receive the mark of the first Beast. **(Rev. 13:11-18; 14:9-11)**

'...The dragon gave him his power, his throne, and great authority...And all the world marveled and followed the beast...' Revelation 13:2b-3b

After being cast out of heaven by Michael the restrainer, Satan will give his power and throne to the Beast. The Beast will have authority over every nation for forty-two months; the second half of the 70th week. **(Rev. 12:6-8; 13:2-5)**

'Then he opened his mouth in blasphemy against God, to blaspheme His name, His tabernacle, and those who dwell in heaven.' Revelation 13:6

He will begin by blaspheming God, His name, His tabernacle and those in heaven. **(Rev. 13:6)** Because of such sacrilege, many Christians will prefer calling him the Antichrist. **(1 John 2:18)**

"These things I have spoken to you, that in Me you may have peace. In the world you will have tribulation; but be of good cheer, I have overcome the world." John 16:33

'...And there shall be a time of trouble, such as never was since there was a nation, Even to that time...' Daniel 12:1

What type of tribulation is our Lord describing? **(John 16:33)** In the New Testament, 'tribulation' can mean distress, pressures of life, affliction, even persecution. Jesus is encouraging us to be hopeful because He has overcome the world. Paul taught tribulation produces perseverance, character, and hope. **(Rom. 5:3-4)** John wrote about the tribulation he and his brothers were suffering. **(Rev. 1:9)** In these instances, tribulation represents distress, trial, and suffering. No believer is exempt. **(2 Tim. 3:12)** While on the Mount of Olives, Jesus spoke of a future 'Great

Tribulation'. **(Mat. 24:21-22, Rev. 7:14)** This will be the most severe persecution the body of Christ will ever experience. **(Dan. 12:1)** Satan's wrath against the saints will begin in the middle of the 70th Week, after the opening of the fourth seal. **(Rev.12:12; Mat. 24:15-22, Rev. 6:7-8)**

15. The Great Tribulation: Satan's Wrath

> The fourth seal is open. Death, the rider of the pale horse, has the power to kill one-fourth of the world. Satan wasted no time in giving the Beast his authority over the nations. The False Prophet was granted the same authority while in his presence.

'I will go up against a land of unwalled villages; I will go to a peaceful people, who dwell safely, all of them dwelling without walls...having neither bars nor gates...' Ezekiel 38:11

In the latter years, God will gather many Jews back to their homeland. **(Ezek. 37:21; 38:8)** The children of Israel will be dwelling safely alongside their enemies during first half of the 70th Week of Daniel. **(Ezek. 38:9-14)** What happens next must have broken Ezekiel's heart. This prophet saw in a vision an unsuspecting Jerusalem being invaded by massive troops. This assault will take place when Israel is a nation, the temple is rebuilt, and the Jewish people will be unsuspecting. **(Dan. 9:27, Mat. 24:15-22)**

'Alas. For that day is great, So that none is like it; And it is the time of Jacob's trouble, But he shall be saved out of it.' Jeremiah 30:7

The prophet Jeremiah calls it, Jacob's trouble. **(Jer. 30:7)** The Great Tribulation will be a time of trouble believers have never experienced. **(Mat. 24:21-22, Dan. 12:1)** In the first half of the week, the Beginning of Sorrows **(Mat. 24:4-8)**, the angel Michael will be restraining the mystery of lawlessness. **(Dan 12:1, 2 Thes. 2:7)** While the killing among the nations rises **(Rev. 6:3-4)**, a complacent Israel will be living in peace. **(Ezek. 38:11, 14)** They will know they've been betrayed when the Abomination of Desolation (Beast) and his ten horns (nations) invade Jerusalem. **(Mat. 24:15, Rev. 17:12-13, Dan. 7:23-25)** A Christ rejecting world won't interfere as another holocaust ravages the Jewish people. **(Luke 21:20-23)**

"For as in the days before the flood, they were eating and drinking, marrying and giving in marriage, until the day that Noah entered the ark and did not know until the flood came and took them all away, so also will the coming of the Son of Man be." Matthew 24:38-39

'For you yourselves know perfectly that the day of the Lord so comes as a thief in the night. For when they say, "Peace and safety!" then sudden destruction comes upon them, as labor pains upon a pregnant woman. And they shall not escape.' 1 Thessalonians 5:2-3

The Beginning of Sorrows, the wars, famines, pestilences, and earthquakes, will cease by the middle of the 70th week. **(Mat. 24:4-8, Rev. 6:1-6)** Assuming the Beast is responsible, the world will be mesmerized by his power. **(Rev. 13:2-4)** This is why the wicked will be declaring peace and safety during the Great Tribulation. **(1 Thes. 5:3, Mat. 24:21-22)** Like the days of Noah, the world will be eating, drinking, and getting married, not knowing their destruction is near. **(Mat. 24:38-39, Luke 17:26-30)** They shall not escape because the Day of the Lord (God's wrath) is coming like a thief in the night. **(1 Thes. 5:2-3)**

"Then they will deliver you up to tribulation and kill you, and you will be hated by all nations for My name's sake. And then many will be offended, will betray one another, and will hate one another." Matthew 24:9-10

"Now brother will deliver up brother to death, and a father his child; and children will rise up against parents and cause them to be put to death." Matthew 10:21

Jesus is giving believers a clear warning of what to expect after the Great Tribulation erupts in the middle of the 70th week. **(Dan. 9:27, Mat. 24:15-22)** Anyone contending for the faith will be hated by all nations. **(Mat. 24:9-10)** Many will be persecuted and killed. **(Rev. 13:1-18)** This is why the price tag for remaining faithful will be too high for most saints. **(Rev. 13:7)** Especially when one's enemies will come from their own household. **(Mat. 10:21)** Many Christians they will betray and hate one another; even causing some to be put to death. Only those obeying the Holy Spirit will be capable of getting the victory over such tribulation. **(Rev. 7:9-14; 15:2)**

"Then many false prophets will rise up and deceive many." Matthew 24:11

"Then if anyone says to you, 'Look, here is the Christ!' or 'There!' For false christs and false prophets will rise and show great signs and wonders to deceive, if possible, even the elect." Matthew 24:23-24

This prophecy is more than frightening. During the Great Tribulation, many false prophets will rise up and deceive many Christians. **(Mat. 24:11)** How will this happen? Anyone believing in their great signs and wonders will be deceived. **(Mat. 24:23-24)** Our Lord isn't saying it's not possible for His elect to be deceived. He is simply emphasizing how deceptive their signs and wonders will be. Even overcomers will have a difficult time discerning they're from Satan. The sign deceiving the entire world will be performed by the second beast. **(Rev. 13:11-14)**

During the Great Tribulation, the False Prophet will make fire come down from heaven.

"And this gospel of the kingdom will be preached in all the world as a witness to all the nations, and then the end will come. Matthew 24:14

"...The harvest is the end of the age, and the reapers are the angels." Matthew 13:39-40

Jesus is telling us the gospel of the kingdom must be preached during the Great Tribulation as a witness to all nations before the harvest can come. (Mat. 24:14, 21-22, 13:39-40, Rev. 14:6-7)

"And because lawlessness will abound, the love of many will grow cold. But he who endures to the end shall be saved." Matthew 24:12-13

Lawlessness will thrive during the days of the Great Tribulation. Because of such chaos, the love of many will grow cold. There is no way of knowing how many will be deceived by the False Prophet. (Mat. 24:12, Rev. 13:11-18) Jesus promises those enduring to the end will be saved. 'Saved' in this passage means physical deliverance. (Mat. 24:12-13, 1 Thes. 5:9) The faithful saints reaching the harvest will be physically saved. (Mat. 13:39-43) Like Noah and Lot, they will be physically delivered before God's wrath is poured out on the wicked. (Luke 17:26-30, Mat. 24:37-39) The Son of Man will send forth His holy angels to gather all overcomers looking up for their physical redemption. (Luke 21:28, 1 Thes. 1:10)

"Therefore when you see the 'abomination of desolation', spoken of by Daniel the prophet, standing in the holy place" (whoever reads, let him understand.' Matthew 24:15

"Then he shall confirm a covenant with many for one week; But in the middle of the week He shall bring an end to sacrifice and offering. And on the wing of abominations shall be one who makes desolate..." Daniel 9:27

The Christ quoted Daniel to teach us two critical truths. **(Dan. 9:27, Mat. 24:15)** The angel Gabriel told Daniel the peace between Israel and her enemies will be broken in the middle of the 70th week. And the leader that breaks this covenant by attacking Jerusalem will be called the Abomination of Desolation. **(Mark 13:14)** So what will happen when we see this deceiver standing in the holy place? Most pastors say it doesn't matter. It matters to our Lord. **(Mat. 24:25)** Those identifying the Abomination of Desolation will know the Great Tribulation has begun. **(Mat. 24:15-22, Rev. 13:5-7)**

"Then let those who are in Judea flee to the mountains. Let him who is on the housetop not go down to take anything out of his house. And let him who is in the field not go back to get his clothes. But woe to those who are pregnant and to those who are nursing babies in those days! And pray that your flight may not be in winter or on the Sabbath." Matthew 24:16-20

The Great Tribulation will not begin in Rome, Moscow, or Washington. As we studied earlier, Satan is going to persecute the woman (Israel) who gave birth to Jesus. **(Rev. 12:13)** After three and a half years of peace, an unsuspecting peaceful people will know they've been betrayed as massive Muslim armies surround Jerusalem. **(Ezek. 38:11, Luke 21:20)** It will be too late once the Abomination of Desolation sits in the temple of God, claiming to be God. **(2 Thes. 2:3b-4)** This is why Jesus gives clear instructions to those living in Judea. They're to flee to the mountains. **(Mat. 24:16)** There won't be time to go back to their house and get more clothes. May this vicious invasion not take place during the winter or on the Sabbath. For the millions fleeing, can you imagine confrontations from those keeping the Sabbath? Or the hardship of those who are pregnant? According to the prophet Zechariah and the apostle John, a third of Israel will flee to a place in the wilderness prepared by God. **(Zech. 13:9, Rev. 12:14)** This unsaved remnant will be protected for the second half of the seven-year week. **(Rev. 12:6)** The same cannot be said for the two-thirds refusing to escape. Eventually, they will be cut off and die! **(Zech. 13:8)**

"For then there will be great tribulation, such as has not been since the beginning of the world until this time, no, nor ever shall be." Matthew 24:21

The Great Tribulation of the saints by the Beast will spread to every nation after the opening of the fourth seal. **(Rev. 6:7-8, Mat. 24:9-26, Rev. 13:5-7)** Martyrs will be seen in heaven after the opening of the fifth seal. **(Rev. 6:9-11; 20:4)** Satan's great wrath will be cut short after Jesus opens the sixth seal. **(Mat. 24:21-22, Rev. 6:12-17, Mat. 24:29)** The same day the Son of Man is revealed **(Luke 17:30)**, a great multitude of believers will come out of the Great Tribulation and stand before the throne of God in heaven. **(Rev. 7:9-17)** Then the seventh seal will be opened. **(Rev. 8:1)** After a half an hour of silence, God's wrath will begin with fire. **(Rev. 8:5-7)**

"And unless those days were shortened, no flesh would be saved; but for the elect's sake those days will be shortened." Matthew 24:22

The False Prophet will attempt to kill anyone refusing to worship the Beast. **(Rev. 13:11-18)** For the sake of His elect, Jesus will shorten this horrific persecution. The gathering of believers at His coming will initiate God's wrath against the wicked that are left behind. **(Mat. 24:21-39)**

'And for this reason God will send them strong delusion, that they should believe the lie.' 2 Thessalonians 2:11

During the days of the Great Tribulation, the wicked will be eating, drinking, and getting married, totally unaware their destruction is near. **(Luke 17:26-30)** And who will be attending their favorite place of worship? Certainly not the overcomers resisting the False Prophet. **(Rev.13:11-18)** Every religion in the world will be worshipping the Beast. After receiving his mark, God will send them a strong delusion because they refused to receive the love of the truth that they might be saved. **(2 Thes. 2:9-12)** No longer able to discern the truth, they'll blindly be thanking the Lawless One for their peace and safety. **(1 Thes. 5:3)**

16. The Two Witnesses

> A stunned world watched as his armies invaded an unsuspecting Jerusalem. The priests shrieked in horror when the Abomination of Desolation defiled their holy place. Jacob's Trouble, the Great Tribulation of the saints, is at hand.

'And I will give power to my two witnesses, and they will prophesy one thousand two hundred and sixty days, clothed in sackcloth.' Revelation 11:3

God will send Two Witnesses to earth the same day the Abomination of Desolation and his armies invade Jerusalem. **(Mat. 24:15, Luke 21:20)** These prophets will prophesy the second half of the 70th week, the same time the Beast has authority over the nations. We aren't told their names nor what they will prophesy. **(Rev. 11:3; 13:5)**

'And if anyone wants to harm them, fire proceeds from their mouth and devours their enemies. And if anyone wants to harm them, he must be killed in this manner. These have power to shut heaven, so that no rain falls in the days of their prophecy; and they have power over waters to turn them to blood, and to strike the earth with all plagues, as often as they desire.' Revelation 11:5-6

How will God empower these prophets? They will be able to stop it from raining, turn water into blood, and strike the earth with plagues. Anyone trying to harm the Two Witnesses will be devoured by fire. **(Rev. 11:5-6)**

'And those who dwell on the earth will rejoice over them, make merry, and send gifts to one another, because these two prophets tormented those who dwell on the earth.' Revelation 11:10

How will their testimony torment those on earth? (Rev. 11:10) Considering the timing of their arrival, these prophets may begin by exposing the evil agenda of the Beast and the False Prophet. (Rev. 11:3; 13:1-18) Surely, sharing the future gathering of believers during the Feast of Trumpets will be a powerful witness. (Mat. 24:30-31, 1 Cor. 15:52) After the resurrection of the elect, the Two Witnesses may warn against the hideous events of the Day of the Lord. (Rev. 8:7-13; 9:1-21; 11:15; 16:1-21) And finally they could prepare the way for the physical return of the Most Holy (Messiah) on the Day of Atonement. (Dan. 9:24, Rev. 10:1-7)

'When they finish their testimony, the beast that ascends out of the bottomless pit will make war against them, overcome them, and kill them. And their dead bodies will lie in the street of the great city which spiritually is called Sodom and Egypt, where also our Lord was crucified.' Revelation 11:7-8

When will they finish their testimony? The Two Witnesses will begin prophesying the same day the Abomination of Desolation declares himself to be God. (Mat. 24:15, 2 Thes. 2:3-4) They will finish their testimony forty-two months later. After the 70th Week is complete, the Beast will kill them. Their ministry will end in the city where our Lord was crucified. (Rev. 11:2-8)

17. First Angel: Preaching The Gospel

> The wars, famines, and earthquakes are no more. The nations are praising the Beast for their peace and safety. The Two Witnesses' warning was barely heard. "The Great Tribulation is underway. This calls for the patience of the saints."

'Then I saw another angel flying in the midst of heaven, having the everlasting gospel to preach to those who dwell on the earth-to every nation, tribe, tongue and people.' Revelation 14:6

On the first day of the Great Tribulation, God will send three angels to those dwelling on the earth. (Rev. 14:6-11)

The first angel will preach the everlasting gospel to every nation.

The second angel will announce the fall of the Harlot.

The third angel will warn not to take the mark of the Beast.

'...That Christ died for our sins according to the Scriptures, and that He was buried, and that He rose again the third day...' 1 Corinthians 15:3-4

'That if you confess with your mouth the Lord Jesus and believe in your heart that God has raised Him from the dead, you will be saved.' Romans 10:9

The gospel is the death, burial, and resurrection of Jesus Christ. All believing in this gospel will be saved. (1 Cor. 15:1-4, Rom. 10:9)

"And this gospel of the kingdom will be preached in all the world as a witness to all the nations, and then the end will come." Matthew 24:14

An angel will begin preaching the everlasting gospel in the middle of the 70th Week. **(Rev. 14:6-7, Mat. 24:14)** He will continue till the gathering of believers to heaven by the Son of Man. **(Mat. 24:29-31, Rev. 6:7-17; 7:9-17)** This is the fulfillment of our Lord's prophecy.

'...And all the world marveled and followed the beast.' Revelation 13:3b

How will the world respond to the gospel angel? Our loving Savior will give everyone an opportunity to hear His everlasting gospel. **(Rev. 14:6)** Instead of believing, the world will be captivated by the Beast. Choosing to obey the False Prophet will be their overwhelming choice. Such a pathetic response is the fruit of many years of brainwashing by Satan. **(Rev. 13:3-18)**

'... "Fear God and give glory to Him, for the hour of His judgment has come; and worship Him who made heaven and earth..." Revelation 14:7

This messenger will exhort the world to fear God and give Him glory. 'Come' in this verse means impending arrival. His divine judgment is coming; it's close. The destruction of sinners will come like a thief in the night. **(Rev. 14:7, 2 Pet. 3:10-12)**

'Those who have the victory over the beast, over his image and over his mark and over the number of his name, standing on the sea of glass, having harps of God.' Revelation 15:2

Who will preach the gospel during the Great Tribulation? The gospel will be preached by an angel **(Rev. 14:6-7)**, by overcomers getting the victory over the Beast **(Rev.15:2)** and possibly the Two Witnesses. **(Rev. 11:2)** They will be a powerful witness before the resurrection at His coming. **(Mat. 24:14; 30-31)**

"But when they persecute you in this city, flee ye into another: for verily I say unto you, Ye shall not have gone over the cities of Israel till the Son of Man come." Matthew 10:23

How will believers living in Israel avoid martyrdom by the False Prophet? They will flee from one city to another; evangelizing along the way. The Son of Man will come back before they reach all the cities of Israel. **(Mat. 10:23; 24:30-31)**

'Let no one deceive you by any means; for that Day will not come unless the falling away comes first, and the man of sin is revealed, the son of perdition.' 2 Thessalonians 2:3

Recently, during a prominent end times conference, several respected teachers prophesied of a major revival during the Great Tribulation. Actually, there is no mention of a revival during Satan's wrath against the saints. It may be just the opposite. There may be more saints overcome by the Beast (Man of Sin) than those getting the victory. **(2 Thes. 2:3, Rev. 13:7; 15:2)**

18. Second Angel: Mystery Babylon Falls

> The first angel is preaching the gospel. The denial by the world is hard to watch. The worship of Satan is preferred. Yet, the overcomers are praising the Lord. They know the gospel has to be preached to all the nations before the harvest can come.

'And another angel followed, saying, "Babylon is fallen, is fallen, that great city, because she has made all nations drink of the wine of the wrath of her fornication..." Revelation 14:8

After the nation of Babylon was destroyed, her pagan religious creed spread around the world. **(Isa. 13:19-22, Jer. 50:39-40)** Since her inception, the mother of harlots has made the nation's drink the wine of her fornication. **(Rev. 17:1-5)** Her demise will be after the Beast seizes control of the nations. **(Rev. 12:12; 13:3-7)** An angel will announce her fall. **(Rev. 14:8)**

'And the ten horns which you saw on the beast, these will hate the harlot, make her desolate and naked, eat her flesh and burn her with fire.' Revelation 17:16

During the Great Tribulation of the saints, the churches of the world will be worshipping the Beast. The wars, famines, earthquakes. and pestilences have ceased. They'll be praising him for their peace and safety. The harlot will no longer be needed. **(Rev. 17:16)** The ten Muslim nations (horns) supporting the Beast will hate her and burn her with fire. **(Rev. 17:12-16; 18:1-24)**

19. Third Angel: Do Not Worship The Beast

> The second angel is declaring the fall of Babylon. The religions of the harlot will no longer make the nation's drink the wine of her fornication. The ten horns of the Beast will hate the harlot. They will make her desolate by burning her with fire.

'Then a third angel followed them, saying with a loud voice, "If anyone worships the beast and his image, and receives his mark on his forehead or on his hand, he himself shall also drink of the wine of the wrath of God..." Revelation 14:9-10a

After the opening of the fourth seal (Rev. 6:7-8), an angel will warn those living during the Great Tribulation not to worship the Beast, his image, or receive his mark. (Mat. 24:21-22, Rev. 7:14; 14:9-11) Anyone who does will drink the wine of the wrath of God.

'He causes all, both small and great, rich and poor, free and slave, to receive a mark on their right hand or on their foreheads, and that no one may buy or sell except one who has the mark or the name of the beast, or the number of his name.' Revelation 13:16-17

Everyone will be given a choice. (Rev. 6:7-11; 14:9-11) No one will be able to buy or sell anything without having the mark of the Beast on their right hand or forehead. We aren't told how long it will take to mark those on earth. (Rev. 13:11-18) The False Prophet will kill anyone refusing to obey. (Rev. 13:15; 20:4)

"And the smoke of their torment ascends forever and ever; and they have no rest day or night, who worship the beast and his image, and whoever receives the mark of his name." Revelation 14:11

The wicked dead are presently suffering in Hades. **(Luke 16:23)** Hades is temporary because it will be cast into the Lake of Fire at the Great White Throne. **(Rev. 20:11-15)** The worshippers of the Beast will be tormented with fire in the presence of the Lamb and His angels. **(Rev. 14:9-10)** The smoke of their suffering will ascend forever. **(Rev.14:11)** Such everlasting punishment can only be Lake of Fire. **(Mat.18:8; 25:46, Rev. 20:15)**

'Here is the patience of the saints; here are those who keep the commandments of God and the faith of Jesus. Then I heard a voice from heaven saying to me "Write: 'Blessed are the dead who die in the Lord from now on. "Yes," says the Spirit, "that they may rest from their labors, and their works follow them." Revelation 14:12-13

The saints are the body of Christ. **(1 Cor. 1:2)** Commandments in this passage means teachings. **(Rev. 14:12-13)** Everyone having faith in Jesus will need patience during the worst persecution the body will ever suffer. We must overcome by the blood of the Lamb and the word of our testimony. Even if we have to give our lives to remain faithful. **(Dan 12:1, Rev. 12:11; 20:4)** Those that die in the Lord will be blessed. Martyrdom will never erase our works in His name. God sees it all. **(Rev. 14:13, Rom. 8:27)**

'And now, little children, abide in Him, that when He appears, we may have confidence and not be ashamed before Him at His coming.' 1 John 2:28

After studying 1 John 2:28, I have two questions. How many will be abiding in Jesus when He appears? And how many will be ashamed because they denied their Lord?

'So they worshiped the dragon who gave authority to the beast; and they worshiped the beast, saying, "Who is like the beast? Who is able to make war with him?" Revelation 13:4

'I was watching; and the same horn was making war against the saints, and prevailing against them.' Daniel 7:21

Can you imagine Christians around the world joyfully waiting in line to receive the mark of the Beast? Such deception didn't happen overnight. Popular wolves will be teaching once a person is saved they can never be lost. **(Acts 20:29, Heb. 3:12)** This is why many saints will believe the lie they can worship the Beast and still keep their crown. **(Rev. 3:11; 13:4-7; 14:11-12)** Nothing could be further than the truth. **(Dan. 7:21)**

20. Fifth Seal: Martyrdom

> The warning from the third angel not to receive the mark of the Beast is being ignored. The priority of most is the survival of families and friends. This is why disobeying the command from the False Prophet is not a viable option for the world.

"Immediately after the tribulation of those days the sun will be darkened, and the moon will not give its light; the stars will fall from heaven, and the powers of the heavens will be shaken." Matthew 24:29

What does Jesus mean by, 'Immediately after the tribulation of those days'? **(Mat. 24:29)** The Lamb will open the first three seals in the first half of the 70th week. **(Mat. 24:4-8, Rev. 6:1-6)** The opening of the fourth seal will initiate the Great Tribulation. **(Rev. 6:7-8, Mat. 24:9-26)** After the fifth seal is opened, martyrs will be seen in heaven. **(Rev. 6:9-11)** Immediately after the tribulation of those days represents the suffering from the first five seals of the heavenly scroll. **(Rev. 6:1-11)**

'When He opened the fifth seal, I saw under the altar the souls of those who had been slain for the word of God and for the testimony which they held.' Revelation 6:9

In the middle of the seven-year week, Michael will cast Satan out of heaven. **(Rev. 12:6-12)** After the fourth seal opens, the Devil will come down having great wrath. **(Rev. 6:7-8)** Satan will grant the Beast his power over the nations for forty-two months. **(Rev. 13:2-7)** Which means the Lamb will open the fifth seal sometime in the second half of the week. **(Rev. 6:9-11)**

'And they cried... "How long, O Lord, holy and true, until You judge and avenge our blood on those who dwell on the earth?"' Revelation 6:10

After the fifth seal opens, there will be souls slain for the word of God and their testimony in heaven. **(Rev. 20:4b)** They're crying out to the Lord to judge those who killed them. These martyrs are asking God to avenge those who killed them after the opening of the fourth seal. **(Rev. 6:7-8, 9-11)**

'Then a white robe was given to each of them; and it was said to them that they should rest a little while longer, until both the number of their fellow servants and their brethren, who would be killed as they were, was completed.' Revelation 6:11

Those killed by the Beast are told to rest until the number of their brethren killed is completed. **(Rev. 20:4b; 6:11)** Which means Satan's wrath against the saints is not over yet. **(Rev. 6:16-17; 15:1)**

'For if we believe that Jesus died and rose again, even so God will bring with Him those who sleep in Jesus.' 1 Thessalonians 4:14

"Then they will see the Son of Man coming in the clouds with great power and glory. And then He will send His angels, and gather together His elect from the four winds, from the farthest part of earth to the farthest part of heaven." Mark 13:26-27

At the opening of the fifth seal, the souls in heaven have not yet received their glorified bodies. **(Rev. 6:9-11)** So, when will their resurrection take place? Jesus will bring the dead in Christ with Him at His coming. **(1 Thes. 4:13-16, Mark 13:26-27)**

21. The Valley Of Jehoshaphat

> The fifth seal is open. The souls slain for the word of God and their testimony are seen under the altar. They're asking how long it will be before their blood is avenged? They're told to rest until the number of their fellow martyrs on earth is completed.

"Let the nations be wakened, and come up to the Valley of Jehoshaphat; For there I will sit to judge all the surrounding nations. Put in the sickle, for the harvest is ripe. Come, go down; for the winepress is full— for their wickedness is great." Joel 3:12-13

Who will God judge in the Valley of Jehoshaphat? From the north is Lebanon and Syria. From the east is Jordan. From the south is Egypt. There are eighteen more nations surrounding Israel desiring the destruction of the Jewish people. Jehoshaphat means the Lord judges. God is going to draw armies from these nations into the Valley of Jehoshaphat to judge them for their wickedness. **(Joel 3:12-13)**

"For the day of the Lord is near in the valley of decision. The sun and moon will grow dark, and the stars will diminish their brightness." Joel 3:15

When will God judge the wicked nations surrounding Israel? **(Zech. 14:12)** Joel prophesied they will be judged just BEFORE the sun, moon, and stars go dark. **(Joel 3:15)** Isaiah saw this same sign BEFORE the Day of the Lord begins. **(Isa. 13:9-10)** Which means our Lord will judge the enemies of Israel BEFORE He opens the sixth seal. **(Rev. 6:12-17, Mat. 24:29)** Once the heavens lose their light, God will punish the world. **(Isa. 13:11)**

'Proclaim this among the nations: "Prepare for war! Wake up the mighty men, Let all the men of war draw near, Let them come up.' Joel 3:9

What invasions are connected to the 70th Week? There will be three wars involving Israel in the last days. These invasions will take place at different times, with different characters, each having a different result. **(Mat. 24:15, Joel 3:9-12, Rev. 16:14-16)**

"But when you see Jerusalem surrounded by armies, then know that its desolation is near." Luke 21:20

The first will be the invasion of an unsuspecting Jerusalem by the Abomination of Desolation after the opening of the fourth seal. **(Dan. 9:27, Mat. 24:15, Luke 21:20, Ezek. 38:9-14, Rev. 6:7-8)**

'And I will show wonders in the heavens and in the earth: Blood and fire and pillars of smoke. the sun shall be turned into darkness, And the moon into blood, Before the coming of the great and awesome day of the Lord.' Joel 2:30-31

The second will be the drawing of Muslim nations into the Valley of Jehoshaphat just before the opening of the sixth seal. **(Joel 2:30-31, Isa. 13:9-11, Rev. 6:12-17, Mat. 24:29)**

'For they are spirits of demons, performing signs, which go out to the kings of the earth and of the whole world, to gather them to the battle of that great day of God Almighty.' Revelation 16:14

The third will be the Word of God and His armies making war against the Beast and his armies at the great day of God Almighty, Armageddon. **(Rev. 16:14-16; 19:11-21)**

22. Sixth Seal: Sun, Moon, and Stars

> The judgment of the nation's surrounding Israel is at hand. Muslim armies are pouring into the Valley of Jehoshaphat. Their wickedness will end just before the heavens go dark. The Jewish people are bracing for another assault. It never came.

'I looked when He opened the sixth seal, and behold, there was a great earthquake; and the sun became black as sackcloth of hair, and the moon became like blood.' Revelation 6:12

"...Therefore if you will not watch, I will come upon you as a thief, and you will not know what hour I will come upon you." Revelation 3:3

The 1970's was a miraculous time for so many inheriting the kingdom of God. I was born again in 1975. From day one, I loved studying eschatology. Anticipating Jesus' return at any moment was so exciting. The Late Great Planet Earth was my favorite book. Yet the more I studied, the more questions I had. Finding answers always led to a frustrating dead end. In 1990, an answer to prayer changed what I always believed. My eyes were miraculously opened to the truth. Understanding the timing of our gathering at His coming is profound, yet so simple. The Day of the Lord will not overtake the overcomers watching for the events of the six seals. **(1 Thes. 5:4, 2 Thes. 2:1-4, Rev. 3:3; 6:1-17)**

"So you also, when you see all these things, know that it is near—at the doors." Matthew 24:33

While on the Mount of Olives, our Lord shared the events that will warn His elect the Coming of the Son of Man is near. John saw these same events. **(Mat. 24:4-33, Rev. 6:1-17)**

First Seal: False teachers deceiving believers.
(Mat. 24:4-5, Rev. 6:1-2)

Second Seal: Wars and rumors of wars.
(Mat. 24:6-7, Rev. 6:3-4)

Third Seal: Famines, pestilences, and earthquakes.
(Mat. 24:7, Rev. 6:5-6)

Fourth Seal: The killing of saints worldwide.
(Mat. 24:9-26, Rev. 6:7-8)

Fifth Seal: Martyrs seen in heaven.
(Mat. 24:9-15, Rev. 6:9-11)

Sixth Seal: Sun, moon, and stars losing their light.
(Mat. 24:29, Rev. 6:12-17)

"Now learn this parable from the fig tree: When its branch has already become tender and puts forth leaves, you know that summer is near." Matthew 24:32

Our Lord used a fig tree to describe the nearness of His coming. **(Mat. 24:32-33)** His disciples knew when the branches of a fig tree become tender and put forth leaves the summer is near. In the same way, believers will know His coming is near when they experience the events from the six seals. **(Mat. 24:4-29, Rev. 6:1-17)**

"And there will be signs in the sun, in the moon, and in the stars; and on the earth distress of nations, with perplexity, the sea and the waves roaring; men's hearts failing them from fear and the expectation of those things which are coming on the earth, for the powers of the heavens will be shaken." Luke 21:25-26

Why the distress of nations when the sixth seal opens? After the sun, moon, and stars go dark, after a great earthquake, after mountains and islands are moved out of place, after the roaring of seas, men's hearts will fail them. **(Luke 21:25-26, Rev. 6:12-17)**

"Assuredly, I say to you, this generation will by no means pass away till all these things take place." Matthew 24:34

'Generation' in this passage is not about a certain number of years. Our Lord is saying the generation (saints) experiencing the events from the six seals will not pass away. Instead, they will see the Son coming in the glory of His Father. **(Mat. 24:29-34)**

"Now when these things begin to happen, look up and lift up your heads, because your redemption draws near." Luke 21:28

In the first half of the 70th week, Jesus will open the first three seals. **(Mat. 24:4-8, Rev. 6:1-6)** He will open the fourth, fifth, and sixth seals in the second half. **(Mat. 24:15, Rev. 6:7-17)** Overcomers will look up for their physical redemption when they see the heavens go dark during the Great Tribulation. **(Luke 21:25-28)** Shrouded in darkness, believers will be gathered by holy angels to heaven before God destroys sinners. **(Mat. 24:29-39, Isa. 13:9-11)**

'... "These are the ones who come out of the great tribulation, and washed their robes and made them white in the blood of the Lamb. Therefore they are before the throne of God, and serve Him day and night in His temple. And He who sits on the throne will dwell among them. They shall neither hunger anymore nor thirst anymore; the sun shall not strike them, nor any heat; for the Lamb who is in the midst of the throne will shepherd them and lead them to living fountains of waters. And God will wipe away every tear from their eyes." Revelation 7:14b-17

How can one prove the Man of Sin will be revealed before the gathering of believers unto Jesus? **(2 Thes. 2:1-4, Mat 24:15-31)** The Beast will begin to war against the saints after the opening of the fourth seal. **(Rev. 6:7-8; 13:5-7)** After the Lamb of God opens sixth seal **(Rev. 6:12-17, Mat. 24:29)**, a great multitude of believers from every nation will come out of the Great Tribulation and stand before the throne of God in heaven. **(Mat. 24:21-22, Rev. 7:14b-17)**

23. The Sign Of The Son of Man

> The heavens shook after the Lamb opened the sixth seal. The sun is black, the moon is blood red, and the stars have no light. The wicked are desperately trying to hide in pitch darkness. They know the wrath of God is coming.

"Then the sign of the Son of Man will appear in heaven, and then all the tribes of the earth will mourn, and they will see the Son of Man coming on the clouds of heaven with power and great glory." Matthew 24:30

While on the Mount of Olives, the disciples asked Jesus what will be the sign of His coming? **(Mat. 24:3)** This sign will look like lighting. Everyone will see Jesus coming on the clouds with power and great glory. **(Mat. 24:27-31, Rev. 1:7)** The Son returning in the glory of His Father will be the sign of the Son of Man. **(Mat. 16:27)**

"Then if anyone says to you, 'Look, here is the Christ!' or 'There!' do not believe it...Therefore if they say to you, 'Look, He is in the desert.' do not go out; or 'Look, He is in the inner rooms.' do not believe it." Matthew 24:23, 26

Saints, we aren't to be fooled. At His coming, the Son of Man will not touch the earth. **(Mat. 24:23-27)** It will be the Most Holy physically returning a second time for the salvation of Israel. **(Dan. 9:24, Acts 1:6-11, Heb. 9:28, Rom. 11:25-27)** Jesus will fulfill these two events during His Second Coming. **(Mat. 24:29-31, Rev. 10:7)**

> **"When it is evening you say, 'It will be fair weather, for the sky is red'; and in the morning, 'It will be foul weather today, for the sky is red and threatening.' Hypocrites. You know how to discern the face of the sky, but you cannot discern the signs of the times." Matthew 16:2-3**

Jesus called the Pharisees hypocrites for not discerning the signs of the times. (Mat. 16:2-3) Sadly, history is repeating itself. Today, most pastors are not watching for the sign of the Son of Man. (Mat. 24:30-33) Instead, they're deceiving many believers with the scare tactic, "Don't be left behind, Jesus could come at any moment." Why is this so evil? When the Son of Man sends forth His angels to gather the righteous, the unrighteous will be worshipping the Beast! (Mat. 24:21-22; 30-31, Rev. 13:2-7)

> **"And to give you who are troubled rest with us when the Lord Jesus is revealed from heaven with His mighty angels, in flaming fire taking vengeance on those who do not know God, and on those who do not obey the gospel of our Lord Jesus Christ." 2 Thessalonians 1:7-8**

At His coming, Jesus will be revealed in flaming fire. He will take vengeance on two types of people. The wicked who do not know God. And those not obeying the gospel of our Lord Jesus Christ. (2 Thes. 1:7-8) Both will be mourning in darkness when they see the sign of the Son of Man. Don't be fooled, no one can obey the gospel without obeying the Holy Spirit! (1 Pet. 4:17, Rev. 2:26-29)

> **'...For the Devil has come down to you, having great wrath, because he knows that he has a short time.' Revelation 12:12**

After the fourth seal, the Devil will attack those having the testimony of Jesus. Even though he only has a short time to deceive, his great wrath will be the worst in history. **(Rev. 12:12-17, Dan. 12:1)** After the sixth seal, Jesus will gather His elect to heaven. Which means the Devil's wrath will begin with the fourth seal and end at the sixth seal. It's that simple. How is it the Devil understands this, yet most Christian's don't? **(Rev. 6:12-17, Mat. 24:21-22, 29-31)**

24. The Coming Of The Son of Man

> The Two Witnesses were predicting the sign of the Son of Man when it happened. Lightning is covering the earth. The wicked are shielding their eyes from the glory of His Father. Overcomers are looking up for their physical redemption.

'Now as He sat on the Mount of Olives opposite the temple, Peter, James, John, and Andrew asked Him privately.' Mark 13:3

While on the Mount of Olives, Jesus shared the events that will warn His coming for His elect is near. (Mat. 24:33) Even though they weren't there that night, Matthew, Mark, and Luke wrote down what He said. (Mat. 24-25, Mark 13, Luke 21) Each received a firsthand account from either Peter, James, John, or Andrew. (Mark 13:3)

"And if I go to prepare a place for you. And if I go and prepare a place for you, I will come again and receive you to Myself; that where I am, there you may be also." John 14:3

The night before His crucifixion, Jesus told His disciples He was returning to His Father's house. (John 14:1-4) They weren't to be troubled. He promised to come back and 'receive' them so they could be with Him forever. This receiving (taken) is His elect being gathered by angels. At the coming of the Son of Man, the righteous will be 'taken' to heaven to receive their rewards at the judgment seat of Christ. Later, they'll be married to the Lamb of God. (Mat. 24:30-31; 16:27, Rev. 19:7)

"Then they will see the Son of Man coming in the clouds with great power and glory. And then He will send His angels, and gather together His elect from the four winds, from the farthest part of earth to the farthest part of heaven." Mark 13:26-27

"Then they will see the Son of Man coming in a cloud with power and great glory. Now when these things begin to happen, look up and lift up your heads, because your redemption draws near." Luke 21:27

At the coming of the Son of Man, the sun, moon, and stars will lose their light. (Mat. 24:29-31, Rev. 6:12-17) Trapped in darkness, the world will see the Son coming on the clouds with the glory of His Father. (Mat. 16:27; 24:27-31) With a great sound of a trumpet, Jesus will send forth angels to gather the dead in Christ. (Mark 13:26-27, 1 Thes. 4:14-16, John 5:28-29) Then a great multitude of overcomers will come out of the Great Tribulation and be caught up with them to be with Lord. (Rev. 7:14, 1 Thes. 4:17) This is the resurrection of believers from the wrath to come. (Luke 21:27)

There is no resurrection when the Holy One returns to finish the mystery of God. (Rev. 10:1-7)

There is no resurrection when the Word wars against the Beast and the False Prophet. (Rev. 19:11-21)

There is no resurrection when the Lamb descends with His Bride! (Rev. 21:9-10)

"For whoever is ashamed of Me and My words in this adulterous and sinful generation, of him the Son of Man also will be ashamed when He comes in the glory of His Father with the holy angels." Mark 8:38

Our Lord is referring to the adulterous sinful generation alive when the Son of Man comes in the glory of His Father. Those ashamed of Jesus and His words will be left behind to suffer His wrath. **(Mark 8:38, Mat. 24:30-39)**

'These are the feasts of the LORD**, holy convocations which you shall proclaim at their appointed times.' Leviticus 23:4**

During His Second Coming, Jesus will fulfill the Feast of Trumpets, the Day of Atonement and the Feast of Tabernacles.

'In a moment, in the twinkling of an eye, at the last trumpet. For the trumpet will sound, and the dead will be raised incorruptible, and we shall be changed.' 1 Corinthians 15:52

The next Feast on God's end-time calendar is the Feast of Trumpets. **(Lev. 23:22-24)** This holy day (Rosh Hashanah) will initiate the Day of the Lord; the last day. **(2 Pet. 3:10, John 6:44, 54)** On this day, the Son will deliver the righteous before punishing the wicked for their iniquity. **(Isa. 13:9-11)** This is our gathering unto Jesus **(2 Thes. 2:1)** before the wrath of the Lamb destroys this Christ-rejecting world. **(Rev. 6:16-17)** Now we know the Son will be revealed the day the Lamb of God opens the sixth seal. **(Luke 17:26-30, Mat. 24:29, Rev 6:12-17)** This is why the heavens will lose their light during the Feast of Trumpets! **(Mat. 24:29-31, Rev. 6:12-17, Isa. 13:10)**

"But of that day and hour no one knows, not even the angels of heaven, but My Father only." Matthew 24:36

Israel's fifth Feast, a memorial of the blowing of trumpets, is called Zikhron Teruah. **(Lev. 23:24, Num. 29:1)** The timing of this holy convocation coincides with the beginning of the new year. According to the Hebrew calendar, the new year will begin with the spotting of a new moon in the seventh month. Every year, Rosh Hashanah (Head of the Year) is celebrated with the blowing of trumpets. This is why many call this ancient observance, the Feast of Trumpets. Due to clouds and a tiny crescent of light of a dark moon, the announcing of the new moon can be difficult. For this reason, this holiday is now two days. No one will know the exact day or hour of the new year until the spotting of the new moon. When Jesus shared 'no one knows the day or hour' of the coming of the Son of Man, His disciples knew He was referring to the fulfillment of the Feast of Trumpets. **(Mat. 24:36)** The prophets call it Israel's dark day, the Day of the Lord. **(Amos 5:18)** On this holy day, the righteous will be delivered before the wicked are punished for their iniquity. **(Isa. 13:9-11)** This horrific judgment will also be used by our Lord to bring unsaved Israel into the New Covenant. **(Heb. 8:8, Rom. 11:25-27, Rev. 10:7)**

"And He will send His angels with a great sound of a trumpet, and they will gather together His elect from the four winds..." Matthew 24:31

During Yom Teruah, 'day of blowing', priests will blow the shofar (rams horn) one hundred times. **(Num. 29:1)** In scripture, God blows the shofar only two times. The first was on Mount Sinai when He revealed himself from heaven in order to bring His people under the Old Covenant. **(Exod. 19:18-20)** When our Lord sounds His last trump, He will send forth angels to gather together believers from heaven and earth. **(Mark 13:26-27, 1 Thes. 4:13-17)** This resurrection will initiate Israel's dark day, the Day of the Lord. **(Mat. 24:30-31, Isa. 13:9-11)**

'And the Lord said to me, "The prophets prophesy lies in My name. I have not sent them, commanded them, nor spoken to them; they prophesy to you a false vision, divination, a worthless thing, and the deceit of their heart.' Jeremiah 14:14**

We have all heard many falsely predict the very day Jesus will come back and gather His elect. They insist they received their prediction from God. (1 Tim. 1:19-20) Let's be clear, the Son of Man will initiate His Second Coming during the Feast of Trumpets. (Mat. 24:30-31, John 6:44) But not this year. Why not? According to our Lord, His resurrection must take place sometime in the second half of the still future 70th week. (Dan. 9:27, Mat. 24:15, 30-31) Nothing can change this revelation.

"For then there will be great tribulation, such as has not been since the beginning of the world until this time, no, nor ever shall be. And unless those days were shortened, no flesh would be saved; but for the elect's sake those days will be shortened." Matthew 24:21-22

"These are the ones who come out of the great tribulation and washed their robes and made them white in the blood of the Lamb." Revelation 7:14

At His coming, the Son of Man will shorten (amputate) the days of the Great Tribulation for the sake of His elect. (Mat. 24:21-31) Between the sixth and seventh seals, a great multitude will be caught up to heaven. (Rev. 7:9-17) They will come out of the Great Tribulation and stand before the Father and the Lamb (Jesus). They're holding palm branches in their hands. They have resurrection bodies. The saints are praising God for their physical deliverance from the wrath of the Lamb! (Rev. 6:16-17; 8:1-7)

Discovering the Events of the Second Coming

'Therefore they are before the throne of God...They shall neither hunger anymore nor thirst anymore; the sun shall not strike them...for the Lamb who is in the midst of the throne will shepherd them and lead them to living fountains of waters. And God will wipe away every tear from their eyes.' Revelation 7:15-17

Why will this great multitude of blood washed believers standing before the throne of God no longer hunger or thirst? It's because they've been delivered out of the Great Tribulation where they weren't able to buy anything without having the mark of the beast. The Lamb is going to wipe away their tears and be their Shepherd. **(Rev. 7:19-17)**

"So you also, when you see all these things, know that it is near..." Matthew 24:33

Can you give an illustration of how the body of Christ will know the coming of the Son of Man is near? **(Mat. 24:33)**

The Beginning of Sorrows will be the labor pangs. **(Mat. 24:8)**
The Great Tribulation will be the hard labor. **(Mat. 24:21-22)**
The gathering of believers will be the delivery. **(Mat. 24:30-31)**

'And Jesus answered and said to them: "Take heed that no one deceives you." Matthew 24:4

"Let no one deceive you by any means..." Paul **(2 Thes. 2:3)**
"Little children, let no one deceive you..." John **(1 John 3:7)**
"Do not be deceived, my beloved brethren." James **(Jam. 1:16)**

For most Christians, heeding warnings not to be deceived is no longer relevant. **(Mat. 24:4)** Such rebellion is producing massive unbelief. **(Luke 18:8)** So how can we prepare to overcome? **(Rev. 12:11)** In his first letter to the Thessalonians, the apostle Paul ends each chapter with a reference to the Second Coming. The emphasis involves our deliverance (1 Thes. 1:10), our hope (2:19), our holiness (3:13), our believing (4:15), and our preservation (Rev. 5:23), at the coming of our Lord Jesus Christ. (2 Thes. 2:1)

'And to wait for His Son from heaven, whom He raised from the dead, even Jesus who delivers us from the wrath to come.' 1 Thessalonians 1:10

'For what is our hope, or joy, or crown of rejoicing? Is it not even you in the presence of our Lord Jesus Christ at His coming?' 1 Thessalonians 2:19

'So that He may establish your hearts blameless in holiness before our God and Father at the coming of our Lord Jesus Christ with all His saints.' 1 Thessalonians 3:13

'For this we say to you by the word of the Lord, that we who are alive and remain until the coming of the Lord will by no means precede those who are asleep.' 1 Thessalonians 4:15

'Now may the God of peace Himself sanctify you completely; and may your whole spirit, soul, and body be preserved blameless at the coming of our Lord Jesus Christ.' 1 Thessalonians 5:23

The righteous will be delivered before the unrighteous suffer God's wrath. How can we be sure? We are to wait for Jesus to deliver us from the wrath to come, the Day of the Lord. (1 Thes. 1:10, 2 Thes. 2:1-4)

'For if we believe that Jesus died and rose again, even so God will bring with Him those who sleep in Jesus.' **1 Thessalonians 4:14**

Besides His angels, who will Jesus bring at His coming? **(Mark 13:26-27)** Although rarely taught, the Son of Man will bring with Him believers that have died throughout history. **(1 Thes. 4:13-15, 1 Thes. 3:13)**

'For the Lord Himself will descend from heaven with a shout, with the voice of an archangel, and with the trumpet of God. And the dead in Christ will rise first.' **1 Thessalonians 4:16**

"Most assuredly, I say to you, the hour is coming, and now is, when the dead will hear the voice of the Son of God; and those who hear will live." **John 5:25**

A body corrupted by sin cannot inherit eternal life. This is why the dead bodies of believers will rise first. We shouldn't marvel at this physical resurrection. **(1 Thes. 4:16)** After hearing His voice, the believers with Jesus will receive their glorified bodies. **(John 5:25)**

'Then we who are alive and remain shall be caught up together with them in the clouds to meet the Lord in the air ...' **1 Thessalonians 4:17**

'Remain' in this passage means survive. Saints surviving the Great Tribulation will be caught up with the dead in Christ to meet their Lord in the air. A great multitude of overcomers will be taken before the throne of God. **(1 Thes. 4:17, Rev. 7:9-17)**

'Now may the God of peace Himself sanctify you completely; and may your whole spirit, soul, and body be preserved blameless at the coming of our Lord Jesus Christ.' 1 Thessalonians 5:23

If a believer can't depart from their faith, then why is Paul praying for believers to be preserved blameless at the coming of our Lord Jesus Christ? **(1 Thes. 5:23)** Why is Jesus stressing the perseverance of the saints till the harvest? **(Mat. 24:13; 13:39)** It's because Satan's wrath won't be cut short until the resurrection of the believers at His coming. **(Rev. 12:12; 7:9-17, Mat. 24:29-31)**

'For this we say to you by the word of the Lord, that we who are alive and remain until the coming of the Lord will by no means precede those who are asleep.' 1 Thessalonians 4:15

"Then the sign of the Son of Man will appear in heaven, and then all the tribes of the earth will mourn, and they will see the Son of Man coming on the clouds of heaven with power and great glory." Matthew 24:30

The main emphasis of Paul's letters is the resurrection of believers. The apostle wrote both letters before the four gospels were written. When Paul spoke 'by the word of the Lord', he was simply repeating Jesus' description of the coming of the Son of Man that was orally passed down by His disciples. Paul calls it the coming of the Lord and the coming of the Lord Jesus Christ. Let's compare each account of His coming.

Will the Antichrist be revealed before His coming? YES
(Mat. 24:15, 2 Thes. 2:1-4)

Are believers exhorted to watch and be ready? YES
(Mat. 24:42-44, 1 Thes. 5:4-6)

Will life be normal at His coming? YES
(Mat. 24:37-39, 1 Thes. 5:3)

Will Jesus come like a thief? YES
(Mat. 24:43, 48-50, 1 Thes. 5:2, 4)

Does Jesus come in the clouds? YES
(Mat. 24:30, 1 Thes. 4:17)

Is a trumpet blown? YES
(Mat. 24:30, 1 Thes. 4:16)

Is there a gathering of dead and alive believers? YES
(Mark 13:26-27, 1 Thes. 4:14-17)

Is there a destruction after His coming? YES
(Mat. 24:37-39, 1 Thes. 5:3)

Is the coming of the Lord taught by Paul (1 Thes. 4:15), the same event as the coming of the Son of Man taught by Jesus (Mat. 24:30-31)? Absolutely!

"See, I have told you beforehand." Matthew 24:25

Jesus is exhorting believers to be watching for the defilement of the holy place by the Abomination of Desolation. (Mat. 24:15, 30-39) Rather than believing this warning, many are trusting in false prophets and false teachers. (Luke 21:8, Mat. 24:11) The hour is late! (John 9:4) Praying for the salvation of lost souls is critical. (Prov. 11:30) We must also warn the vast majority refusing to watch for the Abomination of Desolation. (Mat. 24:15, 33) May the Holy Spirit open their understanding so they can comprehend the danger they're in! (Luke 24:45, Rev. 3:3)

25. The Judgment Seat Of Christ

> The wicked shrieked in terror after seeing the Son of Man coming in power and great glory. At the last trump, angels gathered the dead in Christ and alive overcomers. The Feast of Trumpets is finished. The Second Coming is underway.

"For the Son of Man will come in the glory of His Father with His angels, and then He will reward each according to his works." Matthew 16:27

"When the Son of Man comes in His glory, and all the holy angels with Him, then He will sit on the throne of His glory." Matthew 25:31

'...For we shall all stand before the judgment seat...So then each of us shall give account of himself to God.' Romans 14:10,12

What two events is our Lord highlighting? **(Mat.16:27)** Dead and alive believers will receive their glorified bodies when the Son comes in the glory of His Father with His angels. **(Mark 13:26-27)** After returning to heaven, the Christ will sit upon the throne of His glory and reward each saint according to their works. **(Mat. 25:31)** Paul calls it the judgment seat of Christ. **(Rom. 14:10, 12)**

'For we are His workmanship, created in Christ Jesus for good works, which God prepared beforehand that we should walk in them.' Ephesians 2:10

God has prepared good works for us to walk in. From the moment we are saved until we go to be with our Lord, every good work done for the glory of God will be rewarded at the judgment seat of Christ. **(Eph. 2:10, 1 Cor. 3:11-15, 2 Cor. 5:10-11)** It doesn't matter if man recognizes our works; God does. This is a huge encouragement for us to seek after the mind of Christ. Today, there are many striving after the approval of their pastor, their family, and their friends. Countless others are hopelessly paralyzed by what their peers might think. The lust for such approval, coupled with the fear of man, is so crippling. The evil influence by deceiving spirits in these two strongholds can make us do things we would never do. As believers, we should never allow ourselves to be trapped into coveting the endorsement of man. Such approval means nothing to God. **(Jam. 4:4, Gal. 1:10)**

'For no other foundation can anyone lay than that which is laid, which is Jesus Christ...If anyone's work which he has built on it endures, he will receive a reward.' 1 Corinthians 3:11,14

There is coming a time in heaven **(Rev. 11:18)**, when our Lord will judge the works of glorified believers. All works built on the foundation of Jesus Christ will be rewarded. **(1 Cor. 3:11-14)**

'If anyone's work is burned, he will suffer loss; but he himself will be saved, yet so as through fire.' 1 Corinthians 3:15

Salvation is a gift. His blood washes away our sins because of His grace. **(Rom. 5:18, Eph. 1:7)** Even if all our works are burned up, we will still be spiritually saved. **(1 Cor. 3:15)** That's because no one is saved by performing good works. If salvation could be earned, then Jesus' death would be meaningless. **(Eph. 2:8)** The judging of our works is another story. **(Rev. 11:18)** The reality is our sins, although forgiven, color our works. At the judgment seat all works of the flesh will burn up. Can you imagine the loss we will feel as we watch our selfish works burn up in His presence?

"Whoever therefore breaks one of the least of these commandments, and teaches men so, shall be called least in the kingdom of heaven; but whoever does and teaches them, he shall be called great in the kingdom of heaven." Matthew 5:19

According to our Lord, what will be the outcome of the Judgment Seat? (Mat. 5:19) Although rarely taught, whoever lives and teaches the word of God shall be called great in the kingdom of heaven. Whoever breaks the teachings of Christ and teaches others to do so will be called least. What an awesome inspiration for ministers to proclaim the timing and eternal consequences of the coming of the Son of Man. (Mat. 24, Mark 13, Luke 21) On any Sunday morning, this just isn't happening. (Mat. 7:22)

'My brethren, let not many of you become teachers, knowing that we shall receive a stricter judgment.' James 3:1

The judgment of teachers will be stricter. (Jam. 3:1) The times they refused to teach what the Holy Spirit brought to remembrance will burn up. (John 14:26) The deceptions they sowed that ruined lives will be judged. (Gal. 6:7) Teachers will have to give an account for their refusal to contend for the faith against the wolves bringing destructive heresies denying the Lord. (Jude 1:3, 2 Pet. 2:1)

'For we must all appear before the judgment seat of Christ, that each one may receive the things done in the body, according to what he has done, whether good or bad." 2 Corinthians 5:10-11

Paul taught all must appear before the judgment seat of Christ. **(2 Cor. 5:10-11)** All will be judged for the things they did whether good or bad. What does the apostle Paul mean by, 'we must all appear'? Does he mean all who were ever born, all who are saved, or all who were ever saved? Let's find out.

"No one can come to Me unless the Father who sent Me draws him; and I will raise him up at the last day." John 6:44

"And you will be blessed, because they cannot repay you; for you shall be repaid at the resurrection of the just." Luke 14:14

"Watch therefore, and pray always that you may be counted worthy to escape all these things that will come to pass, and to stand before the Son of Man." Luke 21:36

All believers will be raised up on the last day, the Day of the Lord. **(John 6:44, 1 Thes. 4:15-17)** Jesus calls this the resurrection of the just. **(Luke 14:14)** The saints will stand before the Son of Man and be repaid at the judgment seat of Christ. **(Luke 21:36, Mat.16:27)**

"Do not marvel at this; for the hour is coming in which all who are in the graves will hear His voice and come forth- those who have done good the resurrection of life..." John 5:28-29a

The dead in Christ will hear His voice at His coming. (**John 5:28-29a**) This is the resurrection unto eternal life. (**1 Thes. 4:14-16**) In the twinkling of an eye, their bodies will be raised incorruptible. (**1 Cor. 15:50-52**)

"...And those who have done evil, to the resurrection of condemnation." John 5:29b

'And many of those who sleep in the dust of the earth shall awake, some to everlasting life, some to shame and everlasting contempt.' Daniel 12:2

"I have hope in God, which they themselves also accept, that there will be a resurrection of the dead, both of the just and the unjust." Acts 24:15

There will also be a resurrection unto condemnation. (**John 5:29b**) This is for those who did evil. Daniel calls this judgment shame and everlasting contempt. Many, not all, shall awake at this resurrection. Which means this can't be for all who ever lived. For those who awake, some will receive everlasting life; others everlasting contempt. (**Dan. 12:2, Acts 24:15**) Which means this can't be for all who are saved. This condemnation is reserved for those who were once saved! (**1 Tim. 4:1, 2 Pet. 2:20-22, Heb. 6:4-6**)

"The Son of Man will send out His angels, and they will gather out of His kingdom all things that offend, and those who practice lawlessness." Matthew 13:41

"And I say to you that many will come from east and west, and sit down with Abraham, Isaac, and Jacob in the kingdom of heaven. But the sons of the kingdom will be cast out into outer darkness. There will be weeping and gnashing of teeth." Matthew 8:11-12

At His coming, the Son of Man will send forth His angels to gather out of His kingdom those practicing lawlessness. **(Mat. 13:41)** After the resurrection is completed, many will sit down with Abraham, Isaac, and Jacob in the kingdom of heaven. **(Mat. 8:11-12)** Tragically, before the judgment seat can begin, the sons of the kingdom practicing iniquity will be cast into outer darkness; where there is weeping and gnashing of teeth. **(John 5:29, Mat. 13:39-50)**

"All these things Jesus spoke to the multitude in parables; and without a parable He did not speak to them, that it might be fulfilled which was spoken by the prophet, saying: "I will open My mouth in parables; I will utter things kept secret from the foundation of the world." Matthew 13:34-35

Why are parables by Jesus so important? Parables reveal things kept secret from the foundation of the world. **(Mat. 13:34-35)**

A parable is a simple story highlighting a profound truth. Discovering the meaning is not in the details. It's understanding the main point at the end of each story. The intent is to teach the mysteries of heaven for those having ears to hear. **(Mat. 13:10-16)**

Jesus taught three parables during His Olivet Discourse. Each story tells us what happens AFTER the Son of Man delivers His elect from the wrath to come. **(Mat. 24:45-51; 25:1-13, 14-30)**

The first parable is about a faithful servant who becomes evil while His Master is away. His Master will come back on a day he is not looking for Him; an hour he is not aware of. This evil servant will be given a portion with the hypocrites; where there is weeping and gnashing of teeth. **(Mat. 24:45-51)**

The second parable is about ten virgins. Five are wise and five are foolish. At the coming of the Bridegroom, the wise virgins will enter the kingdom of heaven. The Bridegroom doesn't know the foolish virgins with no oil. These unsaved virgins will not be allowed in. **(Mat. 25:1-13)**

The third parable is about three servants given talents by their Lord. When He comes back, the two servants found faithful will enter into the joy of their Lord. The servant that buried his talent and became wicked is cast into outer darkness where there is weeping and gnashing of teeth. **(Mat. 25:14-30)**

Our Lord concludes with a sheep and goat metaphor. **(Mat. 25:31-46)** After the resurrection of the just and unjust Jesus will sit on His throne of glory and separate His sheep from the goats. **(John 5:28-29, Acts 24:15, Mat. 25:31-32)** Before the righteous give account to their Lord, the wicked will be cast into everlasting fire prepared for the Devil and his angels. **(Mat. 25:41-46; 13:41-42)**

"Then the king said to the servants, 'Bind him hand and foot, take him away, and cast him into outer darkness; there will be weeping and gnashing of teeth." Matthew 22:13

The kingdom of heaven is like a king arranging a marriage for his son. **(Mat. 22:1-13)** While visiting the guests the king finds one without a wedding garment. This man was once a son of the kingdom. **(Mat. 8:11-12)** The king orders this wicked guest be cast into outer darkness. What is this event? It is the everlasting punishment of the unrighteous (goats) before the righteous (sheep) are rewarded at the Judgment Seat of Christ. **(Mat. 25:46)**

"The field is the world, the good seeds are the sons of the kingdom, but the tares are the sons of the wicked one. The enemy who sowed them is the devil, the harvest is the end of the age, and the reapers are the angels. Therefore as the tares are gathered and burned in the fire, so it will be at the end of this age." Matthew 13:39-40

This is the gathering of the sons of the wicked one by angels. The sons of the kingdom practicing lawlessness will be cast into a furnace of fire. **(Mat. 8:11-12)** This isn't the fire of the Day of the Lord. That fire will melt the earth. **(2 Pet. 3:10)** The everlasting fire for the wicked is called the Lake of Fire. **(Mat.13:39-40; Rev. 20:15)**

"Many will say to Me in that day, "Lord, Lord, have we not prophesied in Your name, cast out demons in Your name, and done many wonders in Your name. And then I will declare to them, "I never knew you; depart from Me, you who practice lawlessness." Matthew 7:22-23

Before the judgment of the sheep begins, many practicing lawlessness will be reciting the works they once did in His name. **(Mat. 7:22-23)** It's true, only the redeemed can prophesy correctly, cast out demons, and do many wonders in His name. **(Rom. 12:6, Mark 16:17, Acts 4:29-30)** These crying Lord, Lord, are vainly trying to prove they're still saved. Jesus will tell them I never knew you. 'Knew' represents the intimacy between a man and woman. These practicing lawlessness our Lord never knew intimately. These apostates will be resurrected unto eternal condemnation at the coming of the Son of Man. **(John 5:29, Jude 1:4, Heb. 6:4-6)** They will be cast into everlasting fire originally prepared for the Devil and his angels. **(Mat. 25:41)**

26. The 144,000 Sealed

> The separation of the wicked from the righteous is complete. Their frantic pleas for mercy could not change their fate. The resurrection unto condemnation is over. The sons of the kingdom practicing evil are suffering in everlasting fire.

'And I heard the number of those who were sealed. One hundred and forty-four thousand of all the tribes of the children of Israel were sealed.' Revelation 7:4

What will take place between the sixth and seventh seals? First, a great multitude of saints will come out of the great tribulation and stand before God in heaven. **(Rev. 7:9-17)** After this, 144,000 men from the twelve tribes of Israel will receive the seal of God on their foreheads. **(Rev. 7:2-4)**

'Now a great sign appeared in heaven: a woman clothed with the sun, with the moon under her feet, and on her head a garland of twelve stars.' Revelation 12:1

Who is the woman clothed in the sun? She represents the remnant from Israel that will be protected during the second half of the 70th week. The twelve stars on her head represent the twelve tribes of Israel. **(Rev. 12:1-6; 7:1-8)** After the fullness of the Gentiles is completed, the Lamb will physically gather His redeemed firstfruits (144,000) to Mount Zion. **(Dan. 9:24, Rom. 11:25-27, Rev. 10:1-7; 14:1-4)**

'After these things I looked, and behold, a great multitude which no one could number, of all nations, tribes, peoples, and tongues, standing before the throne and before the Lamb, clothed with white robes, with palm branches in their hands.' Revelation 7:9

During the 70th week of Daniel, how will God deal with Israel and the Church? Throughout history, respected theologians have taught the 70th Week prophecy is only for Israel. They insist God can't deal with the church and unsaved Israel at the same time. Yet, this is exactly what John saw. After the resurrection of overcomers out of the Great Tribulation; 144,000 men from Israel will receive the seal of the living God. These are back to back events, between the sixth and seventh seals, during the second half of the seven-year week. **(Rev. 7:1-8; 9-17)**

'Then I saw another angel flying in the midst of heaven, having the everlasting gospel to preach to those who dwell on the earth—to every nation, tribe, tongue, and people...' Revelation 14:6

The most revered prophecy teachers in the world teach the 144,000 Jewish men will somehow become flaming evangelists after the resurrection of the church. I ask you, how can they evangelize the world when they're hidden away in the wilderness for the second half of the seven-year week? **(Rev. 12:1-17)** The truth is, we aren't told what the 144,000 will do. We do know, the gospel will be preached during the Great Tribulation by an angel, by a great multitude of blood washed saints from every nation, and possibly by the Two Witnesses. **(Rev. 14:6-7; 7:9-17; 11:2-6)**

27. Seventh Seal: Silence In Heaven

> Before His throne, the saints are thanking God. At the same time, an angel reaches the remnant hidden away in the wilderness. The 144,000 are waiting. After receiving the seal of God, they will forever be called the firstfruits of the redeemed.

"Fall on us and hide us from the face of Him who sits on the throne and from the wrath of the Lamb..." Revelation 6:16

Two events will separate the wrath of Satan (Great Tribulation) from the wrath of the Lamb (Day of the Lord). Before the seventh seal is opened, a great multitude will come out of the Great Tribulation and go to heaven before 144,000 Jewish men are sealed by God. (Rev. 7:1-8, 9-17) Neither will suffer the wrath of the Lamb. (Rev. 6:16-17; 8:2; 15:1)

'When He opened the seventh seal, there was silence in heaven for about half an hour.' Revelation 8:1

There will be a half an hour of silence in heaven after the seventh seal opens. Why such a solemn moment? (Rev. 8:1-5) After thirty minutes, God is going to punish the world for its evil. It's called the Day of the Lord. (Isa. 13:9-11)

'I set My rainbow in the cloud, and it shall be for the sign of the covenant between Me and the earth.' Genesis 9:9

What is the sign of the covenant between God and the earth? (Gen. 9:9-17) The rainbow is God's promise not to destroy the wicked with another flood. He never will. In the end, the entire human race will be devoured by fire. **(2 Pet. 3:10-12, Rev. 20:7-9)**

28. The Day Of The Lord's Wrath

> The saints in heaven watched the Lamb open the seventh seal and step away. After a half an hour of silence, an angel filled a golden censor with fire. The Day of the Lord, the punishment of the wicked for their iniquity, is close.

'For the great day of His wrath has come, and who is able to stand?' Revelation 6:17

'The great day of His wrath' is the future Day of the Lord. **(Rev. 6:17, 1 Thes. 1:10, Isa. 13:9)** 'Has come' in this passage is referring to a future event; not a completed action. Remember Judas' betrayal of Jesus in the Garden of Gethsemane? When the traitor arrived with soldiers, Jesus told His disciples His hour 'has come'. Had Jesus faced Pilate? No, His trial was coming. It was in the immediate future. **(Mark 14:41-43)** The seven seals on the heavenly scroll are never called God's wrath. **(Rev. 6:1-17; 8:1)** The only time God will punish the world for its evil and the wicked for their iniquity will be during the sounding of the seven trumpets and the pouring out of the seven bowls. **(Isa. 13:11, Rev. 8:7-13; 9:1-21; 11:15; 15:1; 16:1-21)**

"And this is the will of Him who sent Me, that everyone who sees the Son and believes in Him may have everlasting life; and I will raise him up at the last day." John 6:40

Everyone believing in the Son will be raised up at the last day. The last day is the Day of the Lord. **(John 6:40, 2 Pet. 3:10-12)** The gathering of His elect and the pouring out of His wrath are back-to-back events. **(2 Thes. 2:1-4)** The same day the Son of

Man is revealed in the glory of his Father; the punishment of the wicked will begin. **(Luke 17:26-30, Mat. 16:27)**

'Let no one deceive you by any means; for that Day will not come unless the falling away comes first, and the man of sin is revealed, the son of perdition.' 2 Thessalonians 2:3

Like Noah and Lot, the righteous will delivered before God pours out his wrath on the unrighteous. **(Luke 17:26-30)** Paul highlights two events that must come first. A great falling away of believers and the revealing of the Man of Sin will happen before the Day of the Lord begins. **(2 Thes. 2:1-4)** For the sons of the light watching, this Day will not come as a thief. **(1 Thes. 5:4-7)**

'Multitudes, multitudes in the valley of decision! For the day of the LORD is near in the valley of decision. The sun and moon will grow dark, And the stars will diminish their brightness.' Joel 3:14-15

The heavenly sign preceding God's wrath will be the sun, moon, and stars losing their light. **(Joel 3:14-15, Luke 21:25-27, Mat. 24:29-39)** During this blackout, the wicked will hide from the wrath of the Lamb that is coming. **(Rev. 6:17, Joel 3:14-15, Isa. 13:9-11)**

'Behold, the day of the LORD comes, Cruel, with both wrath and fierce anger, To lay the land desolate; And He will destroy its sinners from it.' Isaiah 13:9

'Then the Lord knows how to deliver the godly out of temptations and to reserve the unjust under punishment for the day of judgment.' 2 Peter 2:9

How will God destroy sinners? **(Isa. 13:9)** The destruction during the Day of the Lord will be unbearable. Mankind doesn't have the power to do such things. **(2 Pet. 2:9; 3:10)** Everyone experiencing the events from the trumpets and bowls will know such wrath can only be from God. **(Rev. 8:1-13; 9:1-21; 15:1; 16:1-21)**

"But take heed to yourselves, lest your hearts be weighed down with carousing, drunkenness, and cares of this life, and that Day come on you unexpectedly." Luke 21:34

The wrath of God will come unexpectedly upon those consumed with the cares of this life. **(Luke 21:34)** No one having the mark of the beast will escape this sudden destruction. **(1 Thes. 5:2-3)** This is why being deceived on when the Day of the Lord begins is not an option for those who want to get the victory over the Beast. **(2 Pet. 3:10-12, Rev. 15:2)**

'Then the angel took the censer, filled it with fire from the altar, and threw it to the earth. And there were noises, thunderings, lightnings, and an earthquake.' Revelation 8:5

Just as the resurrection initiated His Second Coming **(Mat. 24:29-31)**, fire will initiate the Day of the Lord. **(2 Pet. 3:10)** An angel will fill a censor with fire and throw it to earth. **(Rev. 8:5)**

'Then I saw another sign in heaven, great and marvelous: seven angels having the seven last plagues, for in them the wrath of God is complete.' Revelation 15:1

'Then the seventh angel poured out his bowl into the air, and a loud voice came out of the temple of heaven, from the throne, saying, "It is done." Revelation 16:17

When will the Day of the Lord end? The last seven plagues of the wrath of God will be poured out by angels. **(Rev. 15:1)** After the seventh bowl is emptied, a loud voice from heaven will announce His wrath against the wicked is done. **(Rev. 16:17-21)**

'For I testify to everyone who hears the words of the prophecy of this book: If anyone adds to these things, God will add to him the plagues that are written in this book.' Revelation 22:18

'But whoever keeps His word, truly the love of God is perfected in him. By this we know that we are in Him.' 1 John 2:5

What will be the fate of believers adding to The Revelation of Jesus Christ? **(Rev. 22:18)** They will receive the plagues written in the last book in the Bible. **(Rev. 15:1)** It's terrifying hearing ministers teaching John's prophetic letter is merely a picture of good triumphing over evil. They insist the events the apostle saw while on the island of Patmos are just symbolic. In the end, all those adding to the testimony of Jesus Christ will make one crucial mistake. **(Rev. 1:9)** They didn't take Him at His word. **(1 John 2:5)**

29. First Trumpet: Hail And Fire

> Amidst such terror the Two Witnesses' prediction meant nothing. The wicked want out of this nightmare; not another threat. Most are awaiting an answer from their two leaders. The brightness of the sun returning brought them some hope.

'When He opened the seventh seal, there was silence in heaven for about half an hour. And I saw the seven angels who stand before God, and to them were given seven trumpets.' Revelation 8:1-2

When will seven angels be given a trumpet? In the second half of the 70th week, at the opening the sixth seal, the Son of Man will deliver His saints from the wrath to come. (**Mat. 24:29-39, Luke 17:30**) On this same day, He will open the final seal of the heavenly scroll. After a half an hour of silence in heaven; seven angels will each be given a trumpet. (**Rev. 8:1-2**)

'Then another angel, having a golden censer, came and stood at the altar. He was given much incense, that he should offer it with the prayers of all the saints upon the golden altar which was before the throne. And the smoke of the incense, with the prayers of the saints, ascended before God from the angel's hand.' Revelation 8:3-4

Who is praying before the throne of God? An angel holding a golden censor is standing before the altar in heaven. He is given incense to offer with the prayers of the saints before the throne of God. These are the elect gathered by angels at the coming of the Son of Man. (**Rev. 8:3-4, Mark 13:24-27**)

'Then the angel took the censer, filled it with fire from the altar, and threw it to the earth. And there were noises, thunderings, lightnings, and an earthquake. So the seven angels who had the seven trumpets prepared themselves to sound.' Revelation 8:5-6

When will the Day of the Lord begin? **(Isa. 13:9-11, 2 Pet. 3:10)** Once the prayers of the saints ascend before God, an angel will fill a censor from the altar with fire and throw it to earth. The wrath of The Lamb **(Rev. 6:17)**, the destruction of the wicked, will begin with fire. **(Rev. 8:5-6)**

'The first angel sounded: and hail and fire followed, mingled with blood, and they were thrown to the earth. And a third of the trees were burned up, and all green grass was burned up.' Revelation 8:7

What happens after the sounding of the first trumpet? Fire and hail mingled with blood will be thrown to earth. This fire will burn a third of the trees and all the green grass. **(Rev. 8:7)**

"Alas for the day. For the day of the Lord is at hand; it shall come as destruction from the Almighty...O LORD, to You I cry out; for fire has devoured the open pastures, and a flame has burned all the trees of the field." Joel 1:15, 19

The same day the Son is revealed in the glory of His Father, fire will spread throughout the earth. **(Mat. 16:27, Luke 17:30, Joel 1:15, 19, 2 Pet. 3:10-12)** It doesn't say how long this fire will last. We do know the earth will be demolished after the pouring out of the last plague. **(Rev. 15:1; 16:17-21, Isa. 13:9-11)**

30. Second Trumpet: A Sea Of Blood

> Fire from a censor struck the earth. Soon after, the first trumpet sounded. The falling hail set fire to trees and grass on earth. Huge clouds of smoke hugging the ground are like death traps. This punishment for their evil is just the beginning.

'Then the second angel sounded: And something like a great mountain burning with fire was thrown into the sea, and a third of the sea became blood.' Revelation 8:8

After the sounding of the second trumpet, a great mountain burning with fire will be thrown into the sea. The blood from burnt flesh will cover a third of the sea. **(Rev. 8:8)**

'And a third of the living creatures in the sea died, and a third of the ships were destroyed.' Revelation 8:9

During this divine judgment, one-third of the creatures in the sea will die. And a third of the ships will be destroyed. **(Rev. 8:9)**

'But the day of the Lord will come as a thief in the night, in which the heavens will pass away with a great noise, and the elements will melt with fervent heat; both the earth and the works that are in it will be burned up.' 2 Peter 3:10

'And I will show wonders in the heavens and in the earth: Blood and fire and pillars of smoke.' Joel 2:30

Paul, many are teaching only the Middle East will melt during the Day of the Lord. My friends, the flood in Noah's day covered the entire earth. There is no evidence this future destruction will be limited to the Middle East. Only God has the power to rain down fire and smoke upon this Christ rejecting world. Instead of a flood, the earth will be burn up with fervent heat. **(2 Pet. 3:10)** This righteous judging of sinners will be beyond description. **(Isa. 13:9-11)** The smell from blood and smoke will be ghastly. **(Joel 2:30)** Incredibly, this is just the beginning of His wrath. Sometime in the second half of the 70th week (1,260 days), while trees and grass are burning and creatures in the seas are dying, another angel is preparing to sound his trumpet. **(Rev. 8:10-11)**

31. Third Trumpet: Infected Rivers

> The dying sea life is unimageable. Coastal cities saturated with the smell of blood are deserted. The world is pleading with the False Prophet for a miracle. All they can hear is the Two Witnesses warning, 'Only the Lord shall be exalted.'

'Then the third angel sounded: And a great star fell from heaven, burning like a torch, and it fell on a third of the rivers and on the springs of water.' Revelation 8:10

A great star will fall from heaven after the sounding of the third trumpet. It will look like a burning torch. This star will infect a third of the rivers and lakes on earth. (Rev. 8:10)

'The name of the star is Wormwood. A third of the waters became wormwood, and many men died from the water, because it was made bitter.' Revelation 8:11

The name of this star, Wormwood, means bitter.
Anyone drinking this infected water will die. (Rev. 8:11)

"For the day of the Lord upon all the nations is near; as you have done, it shall be done to you; your reprisal shall return upon your own head." Obadiah1:15

What reprisal will the nations receive from God? The infection and death during the Day of the Lord will be an indictment on those refusing to help the children of Israel. All their iniquity will be spewed out upon them. (Obad. 1:12-16)

"Vengeance is Mine, I will repay," says the Lord.' Hebrews 10:30

Should the followers of Jesus ever take vengeance? **(Mat. 5:44)** A great multitude from all the nations will get the victory over the Beast. **(Rev. 7:9-17; 15:2)** But it won't be by physical violence. Their power will come from the blood of the Lamb and the word of their testimony. **(Rev. 12:11)** Only God can repay this world for its wickedness. This is why fellowshipping with militant believers is not an option. Vengeance is mine sayth the Lord! **(Heb. 10:30)**

"For as you drank on My holy mountain, So shall all the nation's drink continually; Yes, they shall drink, and swallow, And they shall be as though they had never been." Obadiah 1:16

How will sinners be remembered? During the Day of the Lord, God will judge the arrogance of the proud. **(Isa. 13:9-11, John 5:26-27)** After drinking the bitter water of Wormwood **(Rev. 8:10-11)**, the accomplishments of the wicked, their legacy, everything they held dear, will disappear and never be remembered. **(Obad. 1:16)**

32. Fourth Trumpet: A Third Of The Sun Struck

> After the third trumpet blast, the wicked saw a star falling like a torch. Wormwood is infecting rivers and lakes around the world. The lifeless bodies lying face down in the bitter water is chilling. Most refused to believe it could get any worse.

'Then the fourth angel sounded: And a third of the sun was struck, a third of the moon, and a third of the stars, so that a third of them were darkened. A third of the day did not shine, and likewise the night.' Revelation 8:12

What is the sign of the fourth trumpet? A third of the sun, moon, and stars will go dark. It doesn't say what will happen during this partial blackout. Neither are we told how long it will last. (Rev. 8:12)

'I looked when He opened the sixth seal, and behold, there was a great earthquake; and the sun became black as sackcloth of hair, and the moon became like blood.' Revelation 6:12

How will the opening of the sixth seal differ from the sounding of the fourth trumpet? (Rev. 6:12-17; 8:12-13)

The sixth seal will open before the fourth trumpet sounds.

The sixth seal will be opened Lamb of God.
The fourth trumpet will be blown by an angel.

At the sixth seal, the heavens will go dark.
At the fourth trumpet, a third of the heavens will lose its light.

At the sixth seal, there will be a great earthquake.
At the fourth trumpet, there is no earthquake.

The sixth seal blackout will come before His wrath.
The fourth trumpet will sound during His wrath.

'And I looked, and I heard an angel flying through the midst of heaven, saying with a loud voice, "Woe, woe, woe to the inhabitants of the earth, because of the remaining blasts of the trumpet of the three angels who are about to sound." Revelation 8:13

After the fourth trumpet sounds, an angel flying in the midst of heaven will warn the inhabitants of the earth. This angelic messenger will declare the final three woes in a loud voice. The remaining blasts from the fifth, sixth and seventh trumpets are about to sound. **(Rev. 8:13; 9:12; 11:15)**

33. Fifth Trumpet: The Bottomless Pit

> The fourth angel sounded his trumpet. Instantly, the sun, moon, and stars lost a third of their light. Parents hiding with their children had no words. No one is listening to the angel flying in heaven. The future three woes are like no other.

'Then the fifth angel sounded: And I saw a star fallen from heaven to the earth. To him was given the key to the bottomless pit. And he opened the bottomless pit, and smoke arose out of the pit like the smoke of a great furnace. So the sun and the air were darkened because of the smoke of the pit.' Revelation 9:1-2

After the fifth trumpet sounds another star will fall from heaven. **(Rev. 9:1-2)** This star represents a fallen angel. He is given a key to the bottomless pit. This may be the same pit Satan will be bound in during the 1,000-year reign of Christ over the nations. **(Rev. 20:1)**

'And they had as king over them the angel of the bottomless pit, whose name in Hebrew is Abaddon, but in Greek he has the name Apollyon.' Revelation 9:11

Who is the angel of the bottomless pit? He is called Abaddon in Hebrew and Apollyon in Greek. **(Rev. 9:11)** His name means destroyer. This evil king can't be Satan because Michael has already cast him out of heaven for the final time. **(Rev. 12:7-12)**

'Then out of the smoke locusts came upon the earth. And to them was given power, as the scorpions of the earth have power.' Revelation 9:3

After Apollyon opens the bottomless pit locusts will come out of the smoke. These foul spirits will have the power to sting like scorpions. God will allow these demons to attack the followers of the Lawless One. **(Rev. 9:3)** All because they refused the love of the truth that they might be saved. **(2 Thes. 2:9-10)**

'They were commanded not to harm the grass of the earth...or any tree, but only those men who do not have the seal of God on their foreheads.' Revelation 9:4

After the gathering a great multitude from the nations to heaven, 144,000 men from the twelve tribes of Israel will receive the seal of the living God. **(Rev. 7:1-8; 9:4)**

'And they were not given authority to kill them, but to torment them for five months. Their torment was like the torment of a scorpion when it strikes a man.' Revelation 9:5

Anyone not having the seal of God will be tormented by these locusts. These demons will not be able to kill. Instead, they will sting like scorpions for five months. **(Rev. 9:5)**

'In those days men will seek death and will not find it; they will desire to die, and death will flee from them.' Revelation 9:6

Why will men prefer death? In the days of the fifth trumpet, the stings from these demons will be excruciating; yet will not lead to death. These constant attacks will be so painful many would rather die than continue to suffer. **(Rev. 9:6)**

34. Sixth Trumpet: A Third Of Mankind Killed

> Apollyon used a key to open the bottomless pit. A horde of demonic locusts emerged from the dark smoke. For five months, they stung the wicked. It was so painful most would rather die than survive such torment. The first woe is past.

'Then the sixth angel sounded: And I heard a voice from the four horns of the golden altar which is before God, saying to the sixth angel who had the trumpet, "Release the four angels who are bound at the great river Euphrates." Revelation 9:13-14

Who will be released when the sixth trumpet sounds? A voice from the golden altar will give the command to release four angels bound at the great river Euphrates. (Rev. 9:13-14) Only unclean spirits, demons, and deceiving spirits are bound in scripture. (Mat. 10:1; 16:17, 1 Tim. 4:1)

'So the four angels, who had been prepared for the hour and day and month and year, were released to kill a third of mankind.' Revelation 9:15

What is their mission? These demons are prepared to kill a third of mankind. (Rev. 9:15)

'Now the number of the army of the horsemen was two hundred million...' Revelation 9:16

Four demons will command an army of two hundred million. **(Rev. 9:15-16)** Most teachers depict this army as human. Are two hundred million soldiers really going to travel to the Euphrates River and kill two billion people? Such a move could take several years. The problem is this horrific slaughter will take place within the second half of the 70th week. Clearly, there isn't enough time to move such a vast human army. This passage is a picture of how hideous it will be when two hundred million demons kill two billion people. **(Rev. 9:17-21)**

'By these three plagues a third of mankind was killed— by the fire and the smoke and the brimstone which came out of their mouths.' Revelation 9:18

Fire, smoke, and brimstone will come out of the mouths of these demons. **(Rev. 9:18)** The earth will eventually melt with fervent heat. The prophets warned mankind of this searing devastation. **(2 Pet. 3:10)** This is why trusting in the scriptures is so key. We aren't to despair over such destruction. Instead, we should be trusting in God's promise of a new heaven and a new earth. **(Rev. 21:1, Isa. 65:17; 66:22)**

'And they were not given authority to kill them, but to torment them for five months. Their torment was like the torment of a scorpion when it strikes a man.' Revelation 9:5

How will the fifth trumpet differ from the sixth trumpet?

The demons from the fifth trumpet will torment the followers of the Beast by stinging them for five months. **(Rev. 9:5)**

The demons from the sixth trumpet will kill a third of mankind. **(Rev. 9:18)**

35. The Death Of The Two Witnesses

> Four angels bound at the Euphrates were released after the sixth trumpet sounded. 200 million demons are ready. Their killing of two billion people is a bloodbath. The Beast was a mere spectator. That changes all now, the second woe is past.

'And I will give power to my two witnesses, and they will prophesy one thousand two hundred and sixty days, clothed in sackcloth.' Revelation 11:3

The Two Witnesses will prophecy 1,260 days; the second half of the 70th Week. **(Rev. 11:3; 12:6, 14)** This is the same time the Beast will have authority over the nations. **(Rev. 13:5)**

'And if anyone wants to harm them, fire proceeds from their mouth and devours their enemies. And if anyone wants to harm them, he must be killed in this manner.' Revelation 11:15

They will have the power to burn their enemies with fire. Those harming them will be killed. **(Rev. 11:5)**

'These have power to shut heaven, so that no rain falls in the days of their prophecy; and they have power over waters to turn them to blood, and to strike the earth with all plagues, as often as they desire.' Revelation 11:6

They will also have the power to stop it from raining, turn water into blood, and strike the earth with plagues. **(Rev. 11:6)**

'When they finish their testimony, the beast...will make war against them, overcome them, and kill them.' Revelation 11:7

Between the sixth and seventh trumpets, the Beast will kill the Two Witnesses. **(Rev. 11:7)** Their testimony will end on the last day of the seven-year week. **(Rev. 11:2-3, Dan. 9:24, Rom. 11:25)**

'And their dead bodies will lie in the street of the great city which spiritually is called Sodom and Egypt, where also our Lord was crucified.' Revelation 11:8

The Two Witnesses will die in the city where our Lord was crucified. **(Rev. 11:8-9)** Their bodies will not be buried. They will lie in a street in Jerusalem for three and a half days. Jerusalem is called Sodom and Egypt because of her rejection of the Messiah for the past two thousand years. Even so, our God promises to protect a believing remnant that survives the Day of the Lord. **(Rom. 11:25-27, Zech. 13:8; 14:2)**

'And those who dwell on the earth will rejoice over them...send gifts to one another, because these two prophets tormented those who dwell on the earth.' Revelation 11:10

The prophecies by the Two Witnesses will torment those on earth. This is why the world may blame the seven trumpet judgments on these anointed messengers. The result will be their rejoicing over their death. In celebration, many will send gifts to each other. It's possible they may think God's wrath is over because the prophets are dead. **(Rev. 11:10)**

'Come, and let us return to the LORD; For He has torn, but He will heal us; He has stricken, but He will bind us up. After two days He will revive us; On the third day He will raise us up, That we may live in His sight.' Hosea 6:1-2

What events will take place in the six days after the completion of the 70th Week of Daniel? **(Dan. 9:24)**

The day the Two Witnesses will finish their testimony at the end of the 70th week, the Beast will kill them. **(Rev. 11:2-7)** As the world rejoices over their death, the Most Holy will physically return on the Day of Atonement (Yom Kippur). **(Dan 9:24, Heb. 9:28, Rev. 10:7)** The Christ will begin by gathering His firstfruits, 144,000, out of the wilderness. **(Isa. 63:1-3)**

On day 2, the Breaker will lead an unsaved remnant on a journey to Jerusalem. **(Mic. 2:12-13, Hab. 3:3-6, 12)**

On day 3, this massive remnant will look upon the Christ and be spiritually saved. Many from Jordan and Egypt will join them on a highway of holiness. **(Hos. 6:1-2, Zech. 12:10; 13:9, Rom. 11:25-26)**

On day 4, the dead Two Witnesses will receive the breath of life from God and ascend in a cloud to heaven. **(Rev. 11:11-12)**

On day 5, the Christ and His remnant will end their magnificent procession into Jerusalem. The Lamb and His firstfruits (144,000) will be celebrating the Feast of Tabernacles atop Mount Zion at the sounding of the seventh trumpet. **(Rev. 11:15-17)** This is when God Almighty will reclaim authority over this earth from Satan. **(Rev. 14:1-4, Obad. 1:21)**

Discovering the Events of the Second Coming

On day 6, Jesus will split the Mount of Olives so His redeemed remnant can safely flee to Azal for protection from the last seven plagues of His wrath. **(Zech. 14:1-5, Rev 15:1; 16:1-21)**

36. The Physical Return Of The Holy One

> The 70th Week is over. The world watched the Two Witnesses die. The partying began when they saw their bodies lying in a lonely street in Jerusalem. Many are celebrating by sending gifts. Social Media is insisting the wrath of God is over.

'That the blessing of Abraham might come upon the Gentiles in Christ Jesus, that we might receive the promise of the Spirit through faith.' Galatians 3:14

If you believe in Christ, you're a rightful heir according to the promise. This is why many Christians call themselves spiritual Israel. We have received the Holy Spirit by faith and have become the spiritual seed of Abraham. **(Gal. 3:13-14, 29)** The problem is some have taken it a step further with devastating consequences. Ministers are teaching the rejection of the Messiah by Israel is permanent. They quote Jesus declaring the house of Israel desolate. **(Mat. 23:37-38)** They believe Israel is no longer God's covenant people. They're convinced the church has replaced Israel. The truth is Gentiles have been grafted into the olive tree meant for the children of Abraham.

'Now when He had spoken these things, while they watched, He was taken up, and a cloud received Him out of their sight. And while they looked steadfastly toward heaven as He went up, behold, two men stood by them in white apparel, who also said, "Men of Galilee, why do you stand gazing up into heaven? This same Jesus, who was taken up from you into heaven, will so come in like manner as you saw Him go into heaven." Acts 1:9-11

During His first coming, the disciples watched Him taken up to heaven in a cloud. **(Acts 1:9-11)** Standing beside them were two angels dressed in white. They told them Jesus will come back the same way He was taken. This will happen when the Christ returns a second time clothed in a cloud. **(Heb. 9:28, Rev. 10:1-7)**

'I saw still another mighty angel coming down from heaven, clothed with a cloud. And a rainbow was on his head, his face was like the sun, and his feet like pillar of fire.' Revelation 10:1

'And the angel answered and said to her, "The Holy Spirit will come upon you, and the power of the Highest will overshadow you; therefore, also, that Holy One who is to be born will be called the Son of God." Luke 1:35

'And in the midst of the seven lampstands One like the Son of Man, clothed with a garment down to the feet and girded about the chest with a golden band. His head and hair were white like wool, as white as snow, and His eyes like a flame of fire; His feet were like fine brass, as if refined in a furnace, and His voice as the sound of many waters.' Revelation 1:13-15

'... "These things says the Son of God, who has eyes like a flame of fire and His feet like fine brass." Revelation 2:18

Who is coming with a rainbow on His head? Between the sixth and seventh trumpets, a mighty Angel will come down to earth clothed in a cloud. **(Rev. 10:1)** Anglos can mean angel, messenger, saint, or holy one. The Holy One has a rainbow on His head. His face is like the sun. His feet like pillars of fire. **(Luke 1:35, Rev. 1:13-15; 2:18)**

'The LORD also will roar from Zion, and utter His voice from Jerusalem; The heavens and earth will shake; But the LORD will be a shelter for His people, And the strength of the children of Israel.' Joel 3:16

'...And he set his right foot on the sea and his left foot on the land, and cried with a loud voice, as when a lion roars...' Revelation 10:2-3

Joel prophesied the Lord will roar from Zion when He comes as a shelter for His people. This will take place when the Holy One roars like a lion after setting one foot on the sea and the other on the land. **(Joel 3:16, Rev. 10:2-3)**

'But in the days of the sounding of the seventh angel, when he is about to sound, the mystery of God would be finished...' Revelation 10:7

'...These were redeemed from among men, being firstfruits to God and to the Lamb.' Revelation 14:4

Standing on the earth, the Holy One will swear by Himself. **(Rev. 10:4-7)** He is announcing there will be no more delay. He will spiritually and physically save a remnant before the sounding of the seventh trumpet. **(Rev. 11:15)** This can't be an angel because only the Lamb of God (Son of God) has the power to finish the mystery of God atop Mount Zion. **(Rev. 14:1-4)**

'For I do not desire, brethren, that you should be ignorant of this mystery...' Romans 11:25

"Seventy weeks are determined, for your people and for your holy city, to finish the transgression, to make an end of sins, To make reconciliation for iniquity, to bring in everlasting righteousness, to seal up vision and prophecy, And to anoint the Most Holy." Dan 9:24

Which mystery is this? (**Rev. 10:1-7**) The apostle Paul is warning believers not to be ignorant of the future salvation of the Jewish people. Once the fullness of the Gentiles ends, our Lord will save a remnant from Israel. (**Rom. 11:25-27, Zech. 14:1-4**) According to the angel Gabriel, Israel must suffer seventy weeks (490 years) of Gentile oppression before the Most Holy returns to make an end of sins and bring in everlasting righteous. (**Dan. 9:24-27, Heb. 9:28**)

'For this is My covenant with them, when I take away their sins.' Romans 11:27

Yom Kippur (Day of Atonement) is the sixth Feast of our Messiah's redemptive career. (**Lev.16:8-34; 23:27-32**) Under the Old Covenant, the High Priest entered the Holy of Holies and made an atonement for sin. The blood sacrifice he offered brought reconciliation between God and the children of Israel. The release of a goat into the wilderness represented the sins of his people. This scapegoat was never to return. This was a shadow (covering) of what is to come. (**Heb.9:7; 8:5-7**)

'But Christ came as High Priest of the good things to come, with the greater and more perfect tabernacle not made with hands, that is, not of this creation. Not with the blood of goats and calves, but with His own blood He entered the Most Holy Place once for all, having obtained eternal redemption.' Hebrews 9:11-12

Under the New Covenant, our High Priest shed His own blood on the cross. The Christ entered the Most Holy Place once and for all; obtaining eternal redemption for all who believe. **(Heb. 9:11-12; 2:17)** When the fullness of the Gentiles is up **(Rom. 11:25-27)**, the Holy One will physically return on the Day of Atonement. **(Heb. 9:28, Dan. 9:24)**

'Therefore, when they had come together, they asked Him, saying, "Lord, will You at this time restore the kingdom to Israel?"' Acts 1:6

Ten days before the Feast of Weeks, Jesus commanded His apostles not to depart from Jerusalem. He wanted them to wait and receive the Promise of the Father. They still asked, "Lord, will You at this time restore the kingdom to Israel?" Jesus made it clear it wasn't for them to know the time. That's because on the day of Pentecost they received the power to become witnesses to the end of the earth. The Promise of the Father is the baptism of the Holy Spirit. **(Acts 1:1-8; 2:1-4)**

'And that He may send Jesus Christ, who was preached to you before, whom heaven must receive until the times of restoration of all things, which God has spoken by the mouth of all His holy prophets since the world began.' Acts 3:20-21

Jesus will not physically return to earth until the restoration of all things begins. **(Acts 3:20-21)** The restoration of the kingdom to Israel is a new heaven and a new earth where God will rule forever. **(Isa. 65:17, 2 Pet. 3:13, Rev. 22:5)** Miraculously, this restoration will begin with the salvation of Israel on the Day of Atonement. **(Acts 1:6-11, Dan. 9:24, Rom. 11:25-27)**

**"For I say to you, you shall see Me no more till you say, 'Blessed is He who comes in the name of the Lord.'"
Matthew 23:39**

During His Second Coming, Jesus will fulfill the mystery of God. (Rev. 10:1-7; 14:1-4) When the children of Israel hiding in the wilderness see Him they will cry out, "Barukh haba b'shem Adonai." (Isa. 63:1-5, Mat. 23:37-39) The Most Holy is coming back a second time to bring in everlasting righteousness. (Heb. 9:28, Dan. 9:24)

'For if you were cut out of the olive tree which is wild by nature, and were grafted contrary to nature into a cultivated olive tree, how much more will these, who are natural branches, be grafted into their own olive tree?' Romans 11:24

How will the Son of Man coming in the glory of His Father differ from the physical return of the Holy One?

"For the Son of Man will come in the glory of His Father with His angels, and then He will reward each according to his works." Matthew 16:27

Between the opening of the sixth and seventh seals, the Son of Man will come in the glory of His Father. (Mat. 24:29-31, Rev. 7:9-17) At the last trump (1 Cor. 15:50-52), the dead in Christ and a great multitude of overcomers will receive their glorified bodies. (1 Thes. 4:13-17, Rev. 7:9-17) Believers will be taken to heaven by angels for the judgment seat of Christ followed by their marriage to the Lamb of God. (Mat. 16:27; 7:21-23, Rev. 11:18; 19:7)

'So Christ was offered once to bear the sins of many. To those who eagerly wait for Him He will appear a second time, apart from sin, for salvation.' Hebrew 9:28

Between the sounding of the sixth and seventh trumpets, the Christ will physically appear a second time. **(Rev. 10:1-7, Heb. 9:28, Dan. 9:24)** The Holy One is returning to fulfill the mystery of God; the salvation of Israel. **(Rom. 11:15-27).**

Jesus will fulfill these two events during His Second Coming.

'Then he shall confirm a covenant with many for one week...' Daniel 9:27a

What part of the year will the Antichrist confirm the seven-year covenant between Israel and her enemies?

The Christ will physically return on the Day of Atonement on the last day of the 70th week of Daniel. **(Rom. 11:25-27, Heb. 9:28, Rev. 10:1-7, Dan. 9:24)** Which means the covenant of peace between Israel and surrounding Muslim nations must begin on or near the Day of Atonement seven years earlier. Every year, Yom Kippur takes place in either September or October. This proves this seven-year week will be confirmed by the Antichrist in the fall of the year. **(Dan. 9:27a)**

37. They Will Look On Me

> While confessing their sins on Yom Kippur, the massive remnant saw Him from afar. A rainbow is on his head. His face is like the sun, His feet like pillars of fire. Men, women, and children cried out, "Barukh haba b'shem Adonai."

'For I do not desire, brethren, that you should be ignorant of this mystery, lest you should be wise in your own opinion, that blindness in part has happened to Israel until the fullness of the Gentiles has come in.' **Romans 11:25**

Days before He gave His life, Jesus declared Jerusalem desolate for killing the prophets sent to her. (Mat. 23:37-39) This rejection created a blindness in which the Jewish people cannot perceive spiritual truth. Their blindness will continue until the fullness of the Gentiles is over. (Rom.11:25-27) At the end of the seven-year week, the Holy One will return on the Day of Atonement and save a remnant from Israel. (Dan. 9:24, Heb. 9:28, Acts 1:6-11, Rev. 10:1-7)

"And it shall come to pass in all the land," Says the LORD, "That two-thirds in it shall be cut off and die, But one–third shall be left in it: I will bring the one–third through the fire, Will refine them as silver is refined, And test them as gold is tested. They will call on My name, And I will answer them. I will say, 'This is My people'; And each one will say, 'The LORD is my God.'" **Zechariah 13:8-9**

Israel will be ready to repent when Jesus physically returns. **(Dan. 9:24, Hos. 5:15)** The affliction of the Jewish people during the 70th week will prepare them to earnestly seek after the Christ. One-third will enter into the new covenant when the Christ returns a second time. **(Jer. 31:31, Heb. 9:28)** Although rarely taught, two thirds will be cut off and die. **(Zech. 13:8-9)**

"And I will pour on the house of David and on the inhabitants of Jerusalem the Spirit of grace and supplication; then they will look on Me whom they pierced. Yes, they will mourn for Him as one mourns for his only son, and grieve for Him as one grieves for a firstborn." Zechariah 12:10

During His wrath, our Lord will pour out a spirit of grace and supplication upon the house of David and the inhabitants of Jerusalem. Those believing will look upon the Holy One their forefathers pierced on a cross. **(Luke 1:35)** The woman (Israel) will grieve as one grieves for a firstborn. **(Zech. 12:10)**

"Who is this who comes from Edom, with dyed garments from Bozrah, This One who is glorious in His apparel, traveling in the greatness of His strength? I who speak in righteousness, mighty to save." Isaiah 63:1

Who is the One glorious in His apparel?
Who is the One traveling in the greatness of His strength?
Who is the One speaking righteousness with the power to save?
In Isaiah's day, Bozrah was the capital of Edom. Today, Edom is the nation of Jordan. The Most Holy will be seen in the Jordanian wilderness wearing dyed garments. **(Isa. 63:1, Dan. 9:24)**

'... "For I have trodden them in My anger, And trampled them in My fury; Their blood is sprinkled upon My garments, And I have stained all My robes."' Isaiah 63:3

Why is blood on His garments? Jesus is wearing garments sprinkled with blood from those suffering His wrath. **(Isa. 63:3)**

"They will call on My name, And I will answer them. I will say, This is My people"; And each one will say, "The LORD is my God." Zechariah 13:9b

After the 70th week ends, the firstfruits having the seal of God will be physically saved. **(Dan. 9:24, Rev. 14:1-4)** The rescue of the 144,000 will begin in the Jordanian wilderness. **(Rev. 12:1-17, Isa. 63:1-3)** Two days later, the massive remnant following Jesus will declare the Lord is my God. **(Hos. 6:1-2, Zech. 13:8-9b)**

'And I will establish My covenant between Me and you and your descendants after you in their generations, for an everlasting covenant, to be God to you and your descendants after you.' Genesis 17:7

What everlasting covenant created the children of Israel? Abraham is the father of the Jewish people. **(Gen. 17:7)** The Abrahamic covenant concerns the land of Israel and the salvation of his future offspring. **(Gen. 12:1-3)** The Mosaic covenant established the Law that would govern Israel. This covenant was fulfilled in the New Covenant. **(Heb. 8:7-9)** Yet, the covenant God cut with Abraham is forever. Gentile believers are not to be ignorant concerning this mystery. Our Lord is going to return on the Day of Atonement. The Deliverer will come out of heavenly Zion and turn away ungodliness from Jacob. **(Rev. 11:26-27)**

'But in the days of the sounding of the seventh angel, when he is about to sound, the mystery of God would be finished...' Revelation 10:7

Our Lord Jesus will gather a remnant from the wilderness on the Day of Atonement. **(Isa. 63:1-3, Dan. 9:24, Rev. 10:1-7)** Five days later, during the Feast of Tabernacles, the Lamb of God fulfill the mystery of God by gathering the final harvest of believers to Mount Zion. **(Rev. 11:15; 14:1-4)**

38. I Will Gather The Remnant

> Deep in the wilderness, the One traveling in the greatness of His strength, mighty to save, poured out the spirit of grace. Their blindness to the gospel is over. Two days before the seventh trumpet, the Lord will seal this remnant from Israel.

'...Behold, the days are coming, says the Lord, when I will make a new covenant with the house of Israel and with the house of Judah.' Hebrews 8:8

A day is coming when our Lord will make a new covenant with Israel. **(Jer. 31:31-33, Heb. 8:8)** The daughter of Zion will be forgiven of her sins. She will be called the holy people; the redeemed of the Lord. **(Isa. 62:11-12)**

"I will surely assemble all of you, O Jacob, I will surely gather the remnant of Israel; I will put them together like sheep of the fold, like a flock in the midst of their pasture; they shall make a loud noise because of so many people." Micah 2:12

During the second half of the 70th week, a third of Israel will be hiding in a place prepared by God. **(Zech. 13:8-9, Rev. 12:6; 11:2)** Once it ends, the Holy One (Messiah) will physically return and gather His remnant. **(Dan. 9:24, Mic. 2:12, Isa. 63:1-4, Zech. 14:1-5)**

"The one who breaks open will come up before them; they will break out, pass through the gate, and go out by it; their king will pass before them, with the LORD at their head." Micah 2:13

Once His firstfruits leave the Jordanian wilderness, the Breaker will be removing any obstacles. **(Mic. 2:13)** The next day the Lord will pass before the remnant of Israel. **(Isa. 11:16)** He will be their head. **(Isa. 63:1-3, Mic. 2:13, Rev. 14:1-4)**

"God came from Teman, the Holy One from Mount Paran. Selah His glory covered the heavens, and the earth was full of His praise. His brightness was like the light; He had rays flashing from His hand, and there His power was hidden. Before Him went pestilence, and fever followed at His feet. He stood and measured the earth; He looked and startled the nations…His ways are everlasting…You marched through the land in indignation; You trampled the nations in anger." Habakkuk 3:3-6, 12

Who will come from Mount Paran?
Who will cover the heavens with His glory?
Who will have rays flashing from His hands?
Who will have pestilence going before Him?
Who will startle the nations?
Who will march through the land in indignation?
Who will trample the nations in His anger?

Habakkuk calls Him the Holy One. Jesus is leading believers from Mount Paran to Mount Zion! **(Hab. 3:3-12, Rev. 14:1-4)**

"They shall walk after the LORD. He will roar like a lion. When He roars, Then His sons shall come trembling from the west; they shall come trembling like a bird from Egypt, Like a dove from the land of Assyria…" Hosea 11:10-11

The Lord will gather His remnant out of the wilderness and march with them to Jerusalem. After hearing His roar, many from Egypt and Jordan will join them on a Highway of Holiness. The Lamb of God will fulfill the Feast of Ingathering (Tabernacles) by gathering this final harvest before the pouring out the last seven plagues of His wrath. **(Hos. 11:10-11, Rev. 14:1-4; 15:1)**

"I will return again to My place Till they acknowledge their offense. Then they will seek My face; In their affliction they will earnestly seek Me." Hosea 5:15

Those seeking His face and acknowledging their offenses against Him, will be redeemed. Our Lord will also physically protect them from His final wrath. **(Hos. 5:15, Rev. 16:1-21)**

'And a rainbow was on his head, his face was like the sun, and his feet like pillars of fire. And he set his right foot on the sea and his left foot on the land, and cried with a loud voice, as when a lion roars...' Revelation 10:1-3

'His eyes were like a flame of fire, and on His head were many crowns...His name is called The Word of God.' Revelation 19:12a-13b

How will the physical return of the Holy One be a different event than the appearing of the Word of God? **(Rev. 10:1-7; 19:11-21)**

The Holy One will return clothed with a cloud.
The Word of God will appear in a robe dipped in blood.
(Rev. 10:1; 19:13)

The Holy One will return with a rainbow on His head.
The Word of God will appear with many crowns on His head.
(Rev. 10:1; 19:12)

The Holy One will set His feet on the earth.
The Word of God will appear in heaven.
(Rev. 10:2; 19:11)

The Holy One will save a remnant from Israel.
The Word of God will war against the Beast and His armies.
(Rev. 10:7; 19:19)

The Holy One will return BEFORE the bowls are poured out.
The Word of God will appear AFTER the bowls are done.
(Rev. 10:1-7; 16:1-21; 19:11-21)

Jesus will fulfill these two events during His Second Coming.

39. The Mystery Of God

> From the wilderness, the Breaker is going before them. He is removing obstacles as believers from Egypt and Jordan arrive. They're coming to celebrate the Feast of Tabernacles. A divine appointment atop Mount Zion no one can stop.

'But in the days of the sounding of the seventh angel, when he is about to sound, the mystery of God would be finished...' Revelation 10:7

Five days before the sounding of the seventh trumpet, the Holy One will physically return to earth and announce the mystery of God is about to be finished. **(Rev. 10:7)** Which mystery is this?

Is it Jews and Gentiles becoming fellow heirs?
Is it the resurrection of believers?
Is it the salvation of a remnant from Israel?

'That the Gentiles should be fellow heirs, of the same body, and partakers of His promise in Christ through the gospel.' Ephesians 3:6

Gentiles becoming fellow heirs in the first century is the mystery Paul highlighted in his letter. **(Eph. 3:1-6)** The church now consists of believing Jews and Gentiles. Both are partakers of the promise in Christ by believing in the gospel. Let's remember, the children of Israel weren't chosen because they were more righteous. God chose them because of His love and mercy. Just like the Gentiles. **(Rom. 9:22-24, 1 Cor. 15:1-4, Tit. 3:4-5)**

> "Behold, I tell you a mystery: We shall not all sleep, but we shall all be changed— in a moment, in the twinkling of an eye, at the last trumpet." 1 Corinthians 15:51

There is another mystery. A corrupted fleshly body cannot inherit the kingdom of heaven. This mystery is the resurrection at the last trump. **(1 Cor. 15:50-52)** This gathering of believers by angels will take place when the Son of Man comes back. **(Mark 13:26-27)** The bodies of the dead in Christ will be raised first. **(1 Thes. 4:13-16, John 5:28-29)** Then a great multitude of overcomers will join them and be supernaturally changed. **(Rev. 7:9-17, 1 Thes. 4:17)**

> 'For I do not desire, brethren, that you should be ignorant of this mystery... that blindness in part has happened to Israel until the fullness of the Gentiles has come in. And so all Israel will be saved...' Romans 11:25-26

Paul wrote of a third mystery. The apostle is exhorting us not to be misinformed about the future salvation of Israel. After the fullness of the Gentiles comes in, a remnant from Israel will be saved by the Christ. **(Rom. 11:25-27, Dan. 9:24, Zech. 13:8-9, Heb. 9:28)**

> "For He said, 'Surely they are My people, Children who will not lie.' So He became their Savior. In all their affliction He was afflicted, And the Angel of His Presence saved them; In His love and in His pity He redeemed them..." Isaiah 63:8-9

When will Israel declare Jesus as their Savior? During His triumphant entry, a multitude lined the road praising the Son of David. It wasn't long before they cried out for His death. **(Mat. 21:8-9; 26:1-2)** Jesus will again return to Jerusalem with a crowd following Him. This time their blindness to the gospel will be removed. The physical descendants of Abraham will be proclaiming Jesus as their Lord and Savior. **(Mat. 23:39, Isa. 63:8-9)**

"A highway shall be there, and a road... called the Highway of Holiness ...The redeemed shall walk there...the ransomed of the LORD shall return...to Zion with singing, with everlasting joy on their heads..." Isaiah 35:8-10

The redeemed will be walking back to Zion on a Highway of Holiness. This highway will pass through parts of Jordan, Israel and Egypt. During their journey to Jerusalem, the King of Kings will be at their head. The ransomed of the Lord will be singing with everlasting joy as they return to Zion! **(Isa. 35:8-10, Mic. 2:14)**

"...On the third day He will raise us up, that we may live in His sight." Hosea 6:2

Three days after the 70th week of Daniel ends, Jesus will raise up a harvest of believers. **(Rev. 10:7, Hos. 6:2)** Just as Moses was given the Ten Commandments on the third day, this remnant from the wilderness will be spiritually saved by the third day. **(Exod. 24:12)** Two days later, they will celebrate the Feast of Ingathering (Tabernacles). **(Isa. 60:14, Rev. 14:1-4)**

40. The Breath Of Life

> The ransomed of the Lord are joyfully singing. They're following their Messiah on a Highway of Holiness. Such an immense ingathering is breathtaking. In the distance is Mount Zion. It is the third day and the Mystery of God is finished.

'Now after the three-and-a-half days the breath of life from God entered them, and they stood on their feet, and great fear fell on those who saw them.' Revelation 11:11

When will the Witnesses receive the breath of life? Our Lord will save His remnant from the wilderness by the third day. By the middle of the fourth day, the Two Witnesses will receive the breath of life. Those watching them rise from the dead will be struck with great fear. **(Hos. 6:1-2, Zech. 13:8, Rev. 11:11)**

'And they heard a loud voice from heaven saying to them, "Come up here." And they ascended to heaven in a cloud, and their enemies saw them. In the same hour there was a great earthquake, and a tenth of the city fell. In the earthquake seven thousand people were killed, and the rest were afraid and gave glory to the God of heaven.' Revelation 11:12-13

Who will see the Two Witnesses ascend to heaven? Their enemies will watch these prophets go up in a cloud. A great earthquake will erupt the same hour. A tenth of the city will fall and seven thousand will be killed. The fearful unsaved will be the ones giving glory to God. **(Rev. 11:12-13; 21:27)**

41. The Lamb On Mount Zion

> Their evil rejoicing lasted three and a half days. The next event is supernatural. After receiving the breath of life, the Witnesses rose to their feet. Their enemies watched them go up in a cloud. Even so, most refused to acknowledge this miracle from God.

'Now the Jews' Feast of Tabernacles was at hand.' John 7:2

'And it shall come to pass that everyone who is left of all the nations which came against Jerusalem shall go up from year to year to worship the King, the Lord of hosts, and to keep the Feast of Tabernacles.' Zechariah 14:16

The Feast of Tabernacles is the final Feast of our Messiah's redemptive career. **(Zech. 14:16, John 7:2)** This celebration is a remembrance of God's protection for those delivered from Egypt. **(Lev. 23:34, Mic. 2:13, Isa. 63:1-3)** It's about the forty years the children of Israel wandered in the desert. Their building of booths (tabernacles) is a reminder of His provision and deliverance. **(Num. 32:13, Neh. 8:14-15)** Sukkot begins after their crops are harvested. For generations the Jewish people have observed this Feast in the City of David, Jerusalem. **(Exod. 34:22; 23:16)**

"And you shall observe the Feast of Weeks, of the firstfruits of wheat harvest, and the Feast of Ingathering at the year's end." Exodus 34:22

The Feast of Tabernacles is also called the Feast of Ingathering. **(Exod. 23:16; 34:22)** Our Lord will fulfill this Feast by gathering His redeemed remnant before pouring out His final wrath. **(Zech. 14:1-5, Rev. 15:1; 16:1-21)** This holy day will begin five days (1,265) after His physical return on the Day of Atonement. **(Rev. 10:1-7; 11:3)**

'Then I looked, and behold, a Lamb standing on Mount Zion, and with Him one hundred and forty-four thousand, having His Father's name written on their foreheads... These are the ones who follow the Lamb wherever He goes. These were redeemed from among men, being firstfruits to God and to the Lamb.' Revelation 14:1, 4

Who will be His firstfruits to God and the Lamb? Just as Jesus was the first to be resurrected and never die; the 144,000 will be the firstfruits redeemed from many Jews. No deceit will be found in their words. In God's eyes, they're without fault. Their Father's name will be on their foreheads. It will be the Lamb who gathers His firstfruits to Mount Zion to celebrate the Feast of Tabernacles. **(Rev. 7:1-8; 14:1, 4, Dan. 9:24)**

'...And I heard the sound of harpists playing their harps. They sang as it were a new song before the throne, before the four living creatures, and the elders; and no one could learn that song except the hundred and forty-four thousand who were redeemed from the earth.' Revelation 14:2-3

From earth, John hears a voice from heaven. Harpists are singing a new song before the throne of God. No one in heaven can learn this song. Only the redeemed 144,000 on earth will be able to. **(Rev. 7:1-8; 14:2b-3)**

42. Seventh Trumpet: He Shall Reign

> The next day, the Lamb of God gathered His firstfruits to the top of Mount Zion. His redemptive career is over. His followers are praising Him for fulfilling the Feast of Tabernacles. To a devastated world, their joyous celebration looked callous.

"The Redeemer will come to Zion, and to those who turn from transgression in Jacob," says the LORD.' Isaiah 59:20

The Redeemer will come to Jerusalem for those turning away from their sin. The 144,000 will celebrate the Feast of Tabernacles with the Lamb of God atop Mount Zion. (Isa. 59:20, Rev. 7:1-8; 14:1-4)

'Then the seventh angel sounded: And there were loud voices in heaven, saying, "The kingdoms of this world have become the kingdoms of our Lord and of His Christ, and He shall reign forever and ever."' Revelation 11:15

Loud voices in heaven will declare it. After the seventh trumpet sounds, Satan will be stripped of his power. The kingdoms of this world will become the kingdoms of our Lord and His Christ. His eternal reign will begin during the Feast of Tabernacles. (Rev. 11:15)

"And in the days of these kings the God of heaven will set up a kingdom which shall never be destroyed; and the kingdom shall not be left to other people; it shall break in pieces and consume all these kingdoms, and it shall stand forever." Daniel 2:44

What will happen in the days of these kings? This is when world leaders will worship the Beast. **(Dan. 2:44, Rev. 17:10-11)** Before making the earth desolate, God will take back the kingdom of this world by spiritually reigning. **(Rev. 11:15)** The Lamb will complete the Feast of Tabernacles BEFORE breaking the kingdom of the Beast into pieces with His final wrath. **(Zep. 1:2-18, Rev. 15:1)**

"Then saviors shall come to Mount Zion to judge the mountains of Esau, and the kingdom shall be the LORD'S." Obadiah 21

Obadiah saw deliverers (saviors) coming to judge after the kingdom (earth) becomes our Lord's. **(Obad. 21, Rev 11:15)** These deliverers are the 144,000 from the twelve tribes of Israel. **(Rev. 7:1-8; 14:1-4)** They may be singing the song of Ascension, Psalm 118, as they ascend Mount Zion to celebrate the Feast of Tabernacles with the Lamb.

'And the twenty-four elders who sat before God on their thrones fell on their faces and worshiped God, saying: "We give You thanks, O Lord God Almighty, The One who is and who was and who is to come, because You have taken Your great power and reigned. The nations were angry and Your wrath has come..."' Revelation 11:16-18a

Lord God Almighty is reigning over a desolate earth. The nations are angry because billions have died. The wicked will know such death and suffering can only be from God. What they don't know is the judgments of the last seven plagues (bowls) will be far greater than the seven trumpets. **(Rev. 11:16-18a; 9:18; 15:1; 16:1-21)**

'And as it was in the days of Noah, so it will be also in the days of the Son of Man: They ate, they drank, they married wives, they were given in marriage, until the day that Noah entered the ark, and the flood came and destroyed them all.' Luke 17:26-27

There are pastors convinced the resurrection at the last trumpet is so obvious. They insist the seventh trumpet has to be the last trumpet. **(1 Cor. 15:52, 1 Thes. 4:16, Rev. 11:15)** This interpretation is false for several reasons. When an angel sounds the seventh trumpet, there is no resurrection of the dead in Christ. There is no gathering of alive believers. The wicked won't be having fun after 200 million demons kill a third of mankind. **(Luke 17:26-27, Rev 9:13-18)**

'So it shall be in that day: The great trumpet will be blown; They will come, who are about to perish in the land of Assyria, And they who are outcasts in the land of Egypt, And shall worship the LORD in the holy mount at Jerusalem.' Isaiah 27:13

The last great trumpet in scripture will sound just before the thousand-year reign of Christ begins. **(Rev. 20:6)** Saved Jews are returning to Zion to worship the Lord. **(Isa. 27:12-13)** During the millennium the Lord will be ruling from the rebuilt House of God of Jacob. **(Isa. 2:1-4)** Clearly, this isn't the resurrection of the elect, which already took place between the sixth and seventh seals. exactly where Jesus places the last trump blown by God! **(Mat. 24:29-31, Rev. 7:9-14, 1 Cor. 15:50-52)**

'In a moment, in the twinkling of an eye, at the last trumpet. For the trumpet will sound, and the dead will be raised incorruptible, and we shall be changed.' 1 Corinthians 15:52

John wrote about the seventh trumpet in 96 A.D. **(Rev 11:15)** Paul wrote about the last trump several decades earlier. **(1 Cor. 15:52)** After studying his letter, the Corinthians understood the last trump during the Feast of Trumpets will initiate God's wrath of the wicked; the Day of the Lord. My friends, with the great sound of a trumpet, the Son of Man will come back on the clouds of heaven with power and great glory after the sun, moon, and stars go dark. **(Mat. 24:29-31, Rev. 6:12-17)**

43. The Mount Of Olives Split

> After the seventh trumpet, Satan lost his power. Loud voices in heaven are proclaiming it. The kingdom of this world has become the kingdom of our Lord and of His Christ. His remnant broke into praise and worship. The third woe is past.

'And in that day His feet will stand on the Mount of Olives, which faces Jerusalem on the east.' Zechariah 14:4

Five days after the Day of Atonement, the Lamb of God and His firstfruits will celebrate the Feast of Tabernacles atop Mount Zion. **(Rev. 10:1-7; 14:1-4)** The next day, Jesus will cross over the Kidron Valley and stand upon the Mount of Olives. **(Zech. 14:4)**

"...And the Mount of Olives shall be split in two...making a very large valley...Then you shall flee through My mountain valley, for the mountain valley shall reach to Azal..." Zechariah 14:4-5

After Jesus splits the Mount of Olives, His remnant will flee through a very large valley to a place called Azal. Azal will be a protected refuge to shield them from His final wrath. **(Zech. 14:2-5, Rev. 15:1)** Most have been taught Jesus will split the Mount of Olives at the supper of the great God. The problem is at Armageddon, the Word of God will appear in heaven. Since Jesus doesn't touch the earth, how can He stand on the Mount of Olives and split it in two? **(Rev. 16:14-16; 19:11-21)**

> "For I will gather all the nations to battle against Jerusalem...But the remnant of the people shall not be cut off from the city. Then the Lord will go forth and fight against those nations, As He fights in the day of battle ... It shall be in that day that I will seek to destroy all the nations that come against Jerusalem." Zechariah 14:2-3; 12:9

The miraculous escape by His redeemed remnant will take place before the first bowl is poured out. **(Zech. 14:2-5, Rev. 16:1-2)** During His final wrath against the wicked, our Lord will gather the nations to battle against Jerusalem. **(Rev. 15:1, Zech. 12:9)** At the battle of Armageddon, Jesus will destroy those that fought against the children of Israel. **(Rev. 16:14-16; 19:11-21)**

> 'The nations were angry, and Your wrath has come, And the time of the dead, that they should be judged, And that You should reward Your servants the prophets and the saints...' Revelation 11:18

When will the prophets and the saints be rewarded? After the seventh trumpet sounds, God Almighty will begin to reign over the kingdoms of this world. **(Rev. 11:15)** Before competing His wrath against His enemies **(Rev. 15:1; 16:1-21)**, Jesus will return to heaven to reward His saints at the Judgment Seat of Christ. Every knee shall bow and every tongue will confess to God before marrying the Lamb. **(Rev. 11:18; 19:7)**

44. The Sea Of Glass

> Leaving Mount Zion, He crossed over the Kidron Valley up to the Mount of Olives. Raising His hands, the mountain spilt in two. Fleeing through a large valley His remnant made it safely to Azal. It is time to destroy those destroying the earth.

'Then I saw another sign in heaven, great and marvelous: seven angels having the seven last plagues, for in them the wrath of God is complete.' Revelation 15:1

After the sounding of the seventh trumpet, John sees in his vision a great and marvelous sign in heaven. Angels having the seven last plagues (bowls) are prepared to complete the wrath of God. **(Rev. 11:15; 15:1; 16:1-21)**

'And I saw something like a sea of glass mingled with fire, and those who have the victory over the beast, over his image and over his mark and over the number of his name, standing on the sea of glass, having harps of God.' They sing the song of Moses, the servant of God, and the song of the Lamb, saying: "Great and marvelous are Your works, Lord God Almighty. Just and true are Your ways, O King of the saints." Revelation 15:2-3

Between the seventh trumpet and the first bowl, the saints will be standing on a sea of glass in heaven. **(Rev. 15:2; 16:1)** These will be the overcomers that get the victory over the Beast during the Great Tribulation. **(Rev. 7:9-14)** They're singing the song of

Moses, the servant of God, and the song of the Lamb; the King of the saints! **(Rev. 15:2-4)**

'After these things I looked, and behold, the temple of the tabernacle of the testimony in heaven was opened. And out of the temple came the seven angels having the seven plagues, clothed in pure bright linen, and having their chests girded with golden bands.' Revelation 15:5-6

After they finish singing, the temple will open. Coming out of the tabernacle are seven angels clothed in pure bright linen having golden bands girded around their chests. **(Rev. 15:5-6)**

'Then one of the four living creatures gave to the seven angels seven golden bowls full of the wrath of God who lives forever and ever.' Revelation 15:7

One of the four living creatures will give each angel a golden bowl full of God's wrath. After this, smoke from the glory of God will fill the temple. **(Rev. 15:7)**

'The temple was filled with smoke from the glory of God and from His power, and no one was able to enter the temple till the seven plagues of the seven angels were completed.' Revelation 15:8

During the trumpet judgments, the temple of God will be open. After seven angels are each given a bowl, the temple will be filled with smoke from the glory of God. No one will be able to enter the temple until these plagues are completed. This is another way to prove the trumpets and the bowls are different events. **(Rev. 11:19; 15:8)**

45. First Bowl: Loathsome Sores

> The saints are standing on a sea of glass singing the song of the Lamb. Suddenly, seven angels clothed in pure bright linen come out of the temple. Each is given a bowl of His wrath. Then the temple was filled with smoke from the glory of God.

'Then I saw another sign in heaven, great and marvelous: seven angels having the seven last plagues, for in them the wrath of God is complete.' Revelation 15:1

'Then I heard a loud voice from the temple saying to the seven angels, "Go and pour out the bowls of the wrath of God on the earth."' Revelation 16:1

A loud voice from the temple will command seven angels to pour out the bowls of the wrath of God. **(Rev.16:1-21)** These last seven plagues will complete the Day of the Lord; the punishment of the world for its evil. **(Rev. 15:1; 16:17, Isa. 13:9-11)**

'So the first went and poured out his bowl upon the earth, and a foul and loathsome sore came upon the men who had the mark of the beast and those who worshiped his image.' Revelation 16:2

Once the first angel pours out his bowl, a foul loathsome sore will come upon every person having the mark of the Beast and those worshiping the image of the Beast. **(Rev. 16:2; 14:9-11)**

'So the angel thrust his sickle into the earth and gathered the vine of the earth, and threw it into the great winepress of the wrath of God. And the winepress was trampled outside the city, and blood came out of the winepress, up to the horses' bridles, for thousand six hundred furlongs.' Revelation 14:19-20

The blood from the followers of the Beast will splatter as high as the horse's bridles. **(Rev. 14:20)** This is a sobering description of the great winepress of the wrath of God. This slaughter will stretch across Israel during the last seven plagues. **(Rev. 15:1)**

"If anyone worships the beast and his image, and receives his mark on his forehead or on his hand, he himself shall also drink of the wine of the wrath of God, which is poured out full strength into the cup of His indignation. He shall be tormented with fire and brimstone in the presence of the holy angels and in the presence of the Lamb." Revelation 14:9-10

Anyone worshiping the Beast shall drink the wine of the wrath of God. His fierce anger will be poured out full strength into the cup of His indignation. The wicked will be tormented with fire and brimstone in the presence of the Lamb and His holy angels. **(Rev. 14:9-10; 20:11-15)**

46. Second Bowl: Sea Creatures Die

> Angels are ready to pour out the last seven plagues. A loud voice from the temple gave the order. The first angel emptied out his bowl. Every follower of the Beast instantaneously received a foul loathsome sore. This plague is beyond hideous.

'Then the second angel poured out his bowl on the sea, and it became blood as of a dead man; and every living creature in the sea died.' Revelation 16:3

The plague from the second bowl will be beyond description. All the creatures in the seas will eventually die. We aren't told how long this bloodbath will take. **(Rev. 16:3)**

'In those days men will seek death and will not find it; they will desire to die, and death will flee from them.' Revelation 9:6

The bowl judgments will be so unbearable, many will prefer death rather than continuing to suffer God's wrath. **(Rev. 9:6)**

47. Third Bowl: Rivers Like Blood

> The oceans are dying. One can see streaks of blood as far as the eye can see. The stench is nauseating. Billions of fish washing ashore is bringing a gory dimension no one can manufacture. God's wrath is destroying the earth's sea life.

'Then the third angel poured out his bowl on the rivers and springs of water, and they became blood.' Revelation 16:4

How will the nations react to the third bowl of His wrath? The sheer panic will be devastating as rivers and lakes spew forth blood with no end in sight. **(Rev. 16:3-4)**

'And I heard the angel of the waters saying: "You are righteous, O Lord, the One who is and who was and who is to be, because You have judged these things."' Revelation 16:5

Jesus is the One who was. **(John 1:29)**
Jesus is the One who is. **(John 5:26-27, Rev. 2:18)**
Jesus is the One who is to be. **(Rev. 21:3-6)**

Our Lord will judge the wicked in a righteous manner. The angel of the waters is praising the One who is, who was, and who is to be. Jesus is the Alpha and Omega, the Beginning and the End, the First and the Last. A pure river of water of life will flow from the throne of God and the Lamb. **(Rev. 16:5; 22:1-13)**

'For they have shed the blood of saints and prophets, and You have given them blood to drink. For it is their just due.' Revelation 16:6

The wicked that shed the blood of the saints and prophets will receive their just due. **(Rev. 16:6, Luke 21:22)**

'And I heard another from the altar saying, "Even so, Lord God Almighty, true and righteous are Your judgments."' Revelation 16:7

Who will be involved in this judgment by God?

The first angel will pour out a plague upon the rivers and lakes. **(Rev. 16:4)**

A second angel will praise the Lord for giving those who shed the blood of the saints their just due. **(Rev. 16:5-6)**

A third angel will declare His judgments are true and righteous. **(Rev. 16:7)**

48. Fourth Bowl: Scorched by Fire

> The third angel poured his bowl into the rivers and lakes and they became like blood. The angel of the waters praised the Lord for giving those who shed the blood of the saints their just due. Another declared this judgment is true and righteous.

'Then the fourth angel poured out his bowl on the sun, and power was given to him to scorch men with fire.' Revelation 16:8

What power will God grant the fourth angel? This angel will be able to scorch men with fire. Like the previous trumpets and bowls, this plague will be worldwide. It doesn't say how long this searing judgment will last. **(Rev. 16:8)**

'And men were scorched with great heat, and they blasphemed the name of God who has power over these plagues; and they did not repent and give Him glory.' Revelation 16:9

During the days of the Great Tribulation, the Beast will blaspheme God, His tabernacle, and those in heaven. **(Rev. 13:6)** All scorched with the great heat after the fourth bowl will also blaspheme the name of God. They're simply modeling the behavior of their leader. **(Rev. 16:9; 13:1; 17:3)**

49. Fifth Bowl: A Kingdom Of Darkness

> After the fourth bowl, this angel was given the power to scorch men with fire. Their screams for mercy were gruesome. Under a strong delusion, they blasphemed His Name. All because they refused the love of the truth that they might be saved.

'Then the fifth angel poured out his bowl on the throne of the beast, and his kingdom became full of darkness; and they gnawed their tongues because of the pain.' Revelation 16:10

In the middle of the 70th Week, Michael will cast Satan out of heaven for the final time. **(Rev. 12:6-12)** Having a short time to conquer, Satan will grant his power over the nations to the Beast. **(Rev. 13:1-7)** After the fifth angel pours out his wrath on the throne of the Beast, his kingdom will be cloaked in darkness. There will be no place to flee for those having his mark. Amidst such torment; they will gnaw their tongues in pain. **(Rev. 16:10)**

'They blasphemed the God of heaven because of their pains and their sores, and did not repent of their deeds.' Revelation 16:11

Because of their constant pain, the followers of the Beast will defiantly blaspheme God. At this point in time it doesn't matter what they say or do. Nothing can stop the righteous punishment of the wicked by a holy God. **(Isa. 13:11)** Even the excruciating pain from the final two bowls will not be able to produce genuine repentance. **(Rev. 16:11-17, 2 Thes. 2:8-12)**

50. Sixth Bowl: Kings From The East

> The fifth angel poured out his plague upon the throne of the Beast. His kingdom is full of darkness. Those having his mark are gnawing their tongues. Such agonizing pain is attracting the spirits of suicide. The wrath of God is almost done.

'Then the sixth angel poured out his bowl on the great river Euphrates, and its water was dried up, so that the way of the kings from the east might be prepared.' Revelation 16:12

The sixth angel will pour out his plague upon the Euphrates River. This great river lines the eastern border of Israel. It is over eighteen hundred miles long. It can be twenty feet deep and a hundred yards wide. God will provide a path for the kings of the east to reach Israel safely by drying up this enormous riverbed. When surviving believers see the great river drying up, they will know the sixth bowl has been poured out. (Rev. 16:12; 19:19)

'And I saw three unclean spirits like frogs coming out of the mouth of the dragon, out of the mouth of the beast, and out of the mouth of the false prophet.' Revelation 16:13

John saw unclean spirits coming out of the mouths of the Dragon, the Beast, and the False Prophet. (Rev. 16:13) This is a clear distinction between three persons. Both deceivers will be suffering in the lake of fire when Satan joins them. (Rev. 19:20; 20:10) This proves Satan is neither the Beast nor the False Prophet.

'For they are spirits of demons, performing signs, which go out to the kings of the earth and of the whole world, to gather them to the battle of that great day of God Almighty.' Revelation 16:14

After the sixth bowl is poured out, three demons will deceive the kings of the earth by performing signs. It will be these unclean spirits who will gather human armies to the battle of the great day of God Almighty. **(Rev. 16:14)**

'And they gathered them together to the place called in Hebrew, Armageddon.' Revelation 16:16

Where will this battle take place? The torment of the wicked will only increase as massive armies from the nation's move toward Armageddon, Israel. In the end, not one follower of the Beast will escape the wrath of God Almighty. **(Rev. 16:16; 19:17)**

'For God has put it into their hearts to fulfill His purpose...until the words of God are fulfilled.' Revelation 17:17

How will God fulfill His purpose? **(Rev 17:17)**

It will be Jesus who dries up the Euphrates River.
It will be Jesus who allows world leaders to be deceived.
It will be Jesus who protects their armies till Armageddon.
It will be Jesus who kills them at the supper of the great God.
(Rev. 16:12-16; 19:17-21)

51. Seventh Bowl: His Wrath Is Done

> It was easy for demons to deceive the kings of the earth. The gathering of armies for the great day of God Almighty is complete. The Euphrates River is drying up. Soldiers are using its dried-up riverbed to reach Armageddon, Israel.

'**Then the seventh angel poured out his bowl into the air, and a loud voice came out of the temple of heaven, from the throne, saying, "It is done." Revelation 16:17**

Once the wrath from the seventh bowl is poured out into the air, a loud voice from heaven will declare, "It is done!" The last seven plagues are finished. **(Rev. 15:1; 16:17)** The Day of the Lord, the punishment of the wicked for their iniquity, is over. **(Isa. 13:9-11, 2 Pet. 3:10)**

'**And there were noises and thunderings and lightening; and there was a great earthquake, such a mighty and great earthquake as had not occurred since men were on the earth...Then every island fled away, and the mountains were not found.' Revelation 16:18, 20**

The greatest earthquake ever will crush the earth. Islands and mountains will be unrecognizable; cities destroyed. **(Rev. 6:18, 20, Ezek. 36:35)** This devastation will be far greater than the earthquake from the sixth seal. **(Rev. 6:12-17)**

'And great hail from heaven fell upon men, each hailstone about the weight of a talent. Men blasphemed God because of the plague of the hail, since that plague was exceedingly great.' Revelation 16:21

How will God will break the kingdom of the Beast into pieces? **(Dan. 2:44)** One hundred-pound hailstones falling from the sky will demolish the earth. In the midst of such annihilation, the wicked will blaspheme God. **(Rev. 16:21)**

'... "Do not weep. Behold, the Lion of the tribe of Judah, the Root of David, has prevailed to open the scroll and to loose its seven seals." Revelation 5:5

Ministers insisting the Second Coming is a single visit are forced to teach the seals, trumpets and bowls are the same events. Saints, we know Jesus will open the seven seals on the outside of the heavenly scroll before seven angels are given trumpets. **(Rev. 5:1-5; 6:1-17; 8:2-6)** And these angels will sound their trumpets BEFORE seven more angels are given bowls. **(Rev. 15:1; 16:1-21)** This clearly proves these twenty-one events are not the same. Nor can they take place simultaneously.

'But the day of the Lord will come as a thief in the night, in which the heavens will pass away with a great noise, and the elements will melt with fervent heat; both the earth and the works that are in it will be burned up.' 2 Peter 3:10

When the Day of the Lord will begin and end? **(2 Pet. 3:10, Rev. 6:16-17)** The wrath of the Lamb will begin with fire after the opening of the seventh seal. **(Rev. 8:1-7)** The Day of the Lord will end after the last seven plagues make the earth desolate. **(Rev. 15:1; 16:17)**

52. The Fate Of Babylon

> Hundred-pound hailstones are destroying everything in sight. Sinners are defiantly blaspheming God. The last seven plagues are complete. A loud voice from the temple is declaring it. The Day of the Lord, the punishment of the wicked, is done.

'And the woman whom you saw is that great city which reigns over the kings of the earth.' Revelation 17:18

'Then you shall again discern between the righteous and the wicked, between one who serves God And one who does not serve Him.' Malachi 3:18

'For the husband is head of the wife, as also Christ is head of the church; and He is the Savior of the body.' Ephesians 5:23

Babylon has always portrayed herself as the true church. From her inception (A.D. 325), the harlot has reigned over the kings of the earth. (Rev. 17:18) So much so, her brainwashed followers will never be able to discern between those serving God and those who aren't. (Mal. 3:18) Only the Christ is the head of the church; the Savior of the body. (Eph. 5:23)

'After these things I saw another angel coming down from heaven having great authority, and the earth was illuminated with his glory. And he cried mightily with a loud voice, saying, "Babylon the great is fallen, is fallen, and has become a dwelling place of demons, a prison for every foul spirit, and a cage for every unclean and hated bird.' Revelation 18:1-2

After illuminating the earth with his glory, an angel having great authority will announce the fall of Babylon. The city of the harlot has become a dwelling place for demons because she made the nation's drunk with the wine of her wrath. (Rev. 18:1-2)

'Now the great city was divided into three parts, and the cities of the nation's fell. And great Babylon was remembered before God, to give her the cup of the wine of the fierceness of His wrath.' Revelation 16:19

After the seventh bowl is emptied, the greatest earthquake ever will divide Rome into three parts. This great city of the harlot will be destroyed before the Word of God wars against the Beast at the great day of God Almighty, Armageddon. (Rev. 16:18-19; 18:1-2; 19:11-19)

'And I heard another voice from heaven saying, 'Come out of her, my people, lest you share in her sins, and lest you receive of her plagues. For her sins have reached to heaven, and God has remembered her iniquities.' Revelation 18:4-5

A voice from heaven will plead with people to come out of the harlot and not share in her sins. (Rev. 18:4-5) Those refusing to obey God will receive the horrific plagues from the trumpets and the bowls. The time has come to remember the iniquities of the mother of harlots. (Rev. 17:5)

'In the measure that she glorified herself and lived luxuriously, in the same measure give her torment and sorrow; for she says in her heart, 'I sit as queen, and am no widow, and will not see sorrow.' Revelation 18:7

What is Mystery Babylon teaching? When the pope declared the Catholic Church is the body of Christ, when he declared he is the Holy Father, when he declared Mary was sinless, when he declared one can go to heaven without believing in Jesus, God was watching. Anyone believing in such heresies does not have God. **(Rev. 18:7, 2 John 1:9)**

'Render to her just as she rendered to you, and repay her double according to her works; in the cup which she has mixed, mix double for her.' Revelation 18:6

My father once shared this story with me. Julio was ten years old when he told his mother he wanted to be a teacher. The word got out. A week later a priest showed up at their home. He told my grandmother it was God's will that Julio become a priest. He threatened this young boy would go to hell if he refused. My father could still remember his weeping mother shaking her head no as the priest stormed out. Even though Julio left the Roman Catholic Church at seventeen, there was still fear on his face when he died at ninety. Like so many threatened by this antichrist cult, my father was still afraid of her. Her punishment for such evil will be double. **(Rev. 17:1-5; 18:6)**

'...Her plagues will come in one day—death and mourning and famine. And she will be utterly burned with fire, for strong is the Lord God who judges her.' Revelation 18:8

Rome will suffer death, mourning, and famine in one day. **(Rev. 18:8)** It will be the Lord God who judges her. During the beginning of sorrows, the voice of the harlot will persuade all faiths to trust the Beast. Can you imagine the persecution of those exposing this evil agenda? Sadly, most don't believe in such spiritual warfare. In their minds, taking a stand against doctrines of demons isn't required. They're hiding behind the excuse only God can judge. They glibly say He has everything under control. It's frightening to see such surrender. Instead of fighting back spiritually most are just rolling over and playing dead. They're rejecting their responsibility to resist the Devil by submitting to God. No one can be a faithful believer and yield to the enemy at the same time. What's happening? Like the Christians living in Nazi Germany during the Holocaust, most living during the Great Tribulation of the saints will choose to remain silent.

'...Alas, alas, that great city Babylon, that mighty city. For in one hour your judgment has come.' Revelation 18:10

How will the great city Babylon be judged? **(Rev. 18:10)** Rome, where the bodies and souls of men were bought, will be destroyed by fire in one hour. **(Rev. 17:5; 18:8-17)**

'The fruit that your soul longed for has gone from you, and all the things which are rich and splendid have gone from you, and you shall find them no more at all. The merchants of these things, who became rich by her, will stand at a distance for fear of her torment, weeping and wailing.' Revelation 18:14-15

The supporters of the harlot always had a greater love for the things of this world. The fruit they longed for will be replaced with torment. Their weeping has nothing to do with repentance. They never had any intention of turning away from their greed. **(Rev. 18:14-15)**

"Rejoice over her, O heaven, and you holy apostles and prophets, for God has avenged you on her." Revelation 18:20

A mighty angel will announce Babylon shall not be found anymore. **(Rev. 18:1-23)** The riches of the city clothed in purple and scarlet are nothing. **(Rev. 17:4; 18:16)** A voice in heaven exhorts the apostles and prophets to rejoice. **(Rev. 18:20)** God has avenged the great city that deceived the nations with her sorcery. **(Rev. 19:1-3)** The fire and smoke rising represents the eternal judgment of Rome. In stark contrast, Jerusalem will become the highest point on earth. **(Isa. 2:2-4)**

'And in her was found the blood of prophets and saints...' Revelation 18:24

Another deception being spread in these last days is the United States is somehow Mystery Babylon.

The problem is:
America isn't a city.
America isn't a religious system.
America hasn't made the nations drunk with spiritual fornication.
America hasn't deceived the world through sorcery.

The frightening truth is the blood of the martyrs of Jesus will be found in the Roman Catholic Church and all her harlots (all man-made religions). **(Rev. 18:24)**

53. The Marriage Of The Lamb

> He remembered the harlot with the fierceness of His wrath. A dwelling place for demons, fire is burning Rome to the ground. In one hour, God avenged this evil city drunk with the blood of the saints. Babylon will never be found again.

"Let us be glad and rejoice and give Him glory, for the marriage of the Lamb has come, and His wife has made herself ready." Revelation 19:7

When and where will the Lamb marry His bride? Five days after the Day of Atonement, Jesus will gather His redeemed remnant to Mount Zion. **(Rev. 10:1-7; 11:15; 14:1-4)** This final harvest is the completion of the Feast of Tabernacles. The next day, Jesus will hide His remnant in Azal for protection from the last seven plagues. **(Zech. 14:4-5, Rev. 15:1)** Before the first bowl is poured out, Jesus will return to heaven. The Christ will sit upon the throne of His glory and reward His glorified saints for their works. **(Mat. 16:27; 25:30-31, 2 Cor. 5:10-11, 1 Cor. 3:8-15)** Once the judgment seat is over **(Rev. 11:18)**, the saints will become His wife. **(Rev. 19:5-7; 21:9-10)**

'... 'Blessed are those who are called to the marriage supper of the Lamb!" And he said to me, "These are the true sayings of God." Revelation 19:9

The marriage supper of the Lamb will be celebrated within the Holy Jerusalem during the 1,000-year reign of Christ over the nations. **(Rev. 19:7-9; 20:6; 21:9-10)** And who will be called to celebrate? It will be the believers dwelling on earth whose names are written in the Lamb's Book of Life. **(Rev. 21:24-27)**

54. The Appearing Of The Word of God

> Arrayed in white linen, His bride is ready. The elders, the living creatures and a host of angels are amazed at her beauty. The voice of a great multitude announces their marriage has come. Blessed are those called to the marriage supper of the Lamb.

'Now I saw heaven opened, and behold, a white horse. And He who sat on him was called Faithful and True, and in righteousness He judges and makes war. His eyes were like a flame of fire, and on His head were many crowns...He was clothed with a robe dipped in blood, and His name is called The Word of God.' Revelation 19:11-13

The blood of the saints has been avenged. A great multitude is praising the Lord for destroying the city of the harlot. (Rev. 17:6; 18:2-21; 19:1-2) The next event is a white horse appearing in heaven. The rider, called Faithful and True, is clothed in a robe dripped in blood. His eyes are like fire. He is wearing many crowns. The Word of God and His armies are returning to war against the Beast and his armies. (Rev. 19:11-21)

'Now out of His mouth goes a sharp sword, that with it He should strike the nations...He Himself treads the winepress of the fierceness and wrath of Almighty God. And He has on His robe and on His thigh a name written: KING OF KINGS AND LORD OF LORDS.' Revelation 19:15-16

Only the Word of God has the power to tread the winepress of the wrath of Almighty God. The King of Kings and Lord of Lords is going to strike the nations with a sharp sword. **(Rev. 19:15-16)**

'And to her it was granted to be arrayed in fine linen, clean and bright, for the fine linen is the righteous acts of the saints.' Revelation 19:8

'And the armies in heaven, clothed in fine linen, white and clean, followed Him on white horses.' Revelation 19:14

'And out of the temple came the seven angels having the seven plagues, clothed in pure bright linen, and having their chests girded with golden bands.' Revelation 15:6

The white fine linen the bride is wearing at her marriage represents her righteous acts. **(Rev. 19:8)** The armies following the Word of God are also clothed in fine white linen. **(Rev. 19:14)** This is why many teach His armies will be the bride of Christ. Yet, angels are also clothed in pure bright linen. **(Rev. 15:6, Acts 1:10)** Clearly, the bride will return to earth only one time. This will happen when the Lamb and His bride return on the first day of their 1,000-year reign over the nations. **(Rev. 21:2-10)** Which means the armies following the Word of God will be angels clothed in fine white linen.

"Then he shall confirm a covenant with many for one week; But in the middle of the week He shall bring an end to sacrifice and offering. And on the wing of abominations shall be one who makes desolate...until the consummation, which is determined, is poured out on the desolate." Daniel 9:27

"And from the time that the daily sacrifice is taken away, and the abomination of desolation is set up, there shall be one thousand two hundred and ninety days." Daniel 12:11

From the defiling of the holy place by the Abomination of Desolation (Mat. 24:15), till the end of the seven-year week, there will be 1,260 days. (Rev. 12:6) According to Daniel, this deceiver will become desolate thirty days later (1,290 days). (Dan. 9:27; 12:11) Now we know the Beast will become desolate at the supper of the great God. (Rev. 19:11-21) Which means from the middle of the 70th week, till Jesus casts the Beast into the lake of fire, there will be 1,290 days. (Dan. 12:11, Rev. 16:14-16)

'...These two were cast alive into the lake of fire burning with brimstone.' Revelation 19:20

At the end of the second half of the seven-year week (1,260 days), the Holy One will return on the Day of Atonement. (Dan. 9:24, Heb. 9:28, Rev. 10:17) Thirty days later, the Word of God and His armies of angels will appear in heaven. (Rev. 19:11-21; Dan.12:11)

'...Come and gather together for the supper of the great God, that you may eat the flesh of kings...the flesh of mighty men, the flesh of horses and of those who sit on them, the flesh of all people, free and slave, both small and great.' Revelation 19:17b-18

An angel standing in the sun will cry out to birds to gather together for the supper of the great God. They're coming to eat the flesh of dead men and horses. And where will this slaughter take place? The Beast and his armies will gather at Armageddon, Israel. (Rev. 19:17b-18; 16:14-16)

'And the rest were killed with the sword which proceeded from the mouth of Him who sat on the horse. And all the birds were filled with their flesh.' Revelation 19:21

After the two beasts are cast alive into the lake of fire, the Word of God will kill their followers with a sword. Their blood will be splattered as high as the horse's bridles. Then the birds will eat their flesh. This is the fulfillment of His promise to punish the world for its evil and the wicked for their iniquity. The great winepress of the wrath of God is over. **(Rev. 14:18-20; 19:20-21, Isa. 13:9-11)**

'Behold I am coming as a thief. Blessed is he who watches, and keeps his garments, lest he walk naked and they see his shame.' Revelation 16:15

In the New Testament, the five references of Jesus coming back as a thief concerns the resurrection of the elect. **(1 Thes. 5:2, 4, 2 Pet. 3:10, Rev. 3:3; 16:15)** When the Son comes in the glory of His Father it will be like the days of Noah and Lot. **(Mat. 24:30-39)** The wicked will be eating, drinking, and getting married, totally unaware their destruction is near. **(Luke 12:38-40, 1 Thes. 5:2-4)** The day the Son of Man is revealed the righteous will be taken and the unrighteous will be left. **(Luke 17:26-30, Mat. 24:40-41)**

When the Word of God arrives on a white horse to wage war against the Beast and his armies, two-thirds of mankind will be dead. **(Rev. 9:17-18)** The oceans, rivers, and lakes will be infected. The followers of the Beast will be gnawing in pain from their sores. **(Rev. 16:1-2)** No one will be having fun on the eve of Armageddon. **(Rev. 16:14-16)**

Jesus won't be coming as a thief in the night to a demolished world. This will ONLY happen when angels gather believers out of the Great Tribulation at the coming of the Son of Man. **(Mat. 24:21-31, Rev. 7:14-17)** The truth is, none of the things that take place during the coming of the Son of Man will take place during the appearing of the Word of God. These are two different events Jesus will fulfill during His Second Coming. **(Mat. 24:30-31, Rev. 19:11-21)**

55. The Mountain Of The Lord's House

> They saw the appearing of the Word of God and His armies. The Beast and False Prophet were cast alive into the lake of fire before Jesus killed their followers in righteous anger. Birds are feasting on their flesh at the supper of the great God.

'Blessed is he who waits and comes to the one thousand three hundred and thirty-five days.' Daniel 12:12

There will be forty-five days from Armageddon (1,290 days) till the first day of Christ's 1,000-year reign over the nations (1,335 days). Four events will take place within this forty-five-day period. **(Dan. 12:11-12, Rev. 20:6; 21:9-10)**

1. Jerusalem will become the highest point on earth. **(Isa. 2:2-4)**
2. A redeemed remnant from Israel will return. **(Isa. 10:20-21)**
3. Surviving Gentiles will be gathered to Jerusalem. **(Isa. 66:18-19)**
4. The temple will be built by our Lord. **(Zech. 6:12-13)**

"Now it shall come to pass in the latter days that the mountain of the Lord's house shall be established on the top of the mountains. And all nations shall flow to it." Isaiah 2:2

The first event after the slaughter at Armageddon will be the establishment of Jerusalem to the highest point on earth. Isaiah prophesied the Lord's house will be established on the top of the mountains. **(Isa. 2:2, Zech. 8:8, 22; 6:12-13)**

"And it shall come to pass that everyone who is left of all the nations which came against Jerusalem shall go up from year to year to worship the King, the LORD of hosts, and to keep the Feast of Tabernacles." Zechariah 14:16

During the 1,000-year reign of Christ, those who came against Jerusalem will be worshiping the King. **(Zech. 14:16, Rev. 20:6)** Their worship during the Feast of Tabernacles will be atop the highest point on earth; the Mountain of the Lord. **(Isa. 2:2)**

'... "Come, and let us go up to the mountain of the LORD, to the house of the God of Jacob; He will teach us His ways, and we shall walk in His paths." For out of Zion shall go forth the law, and the word of the LORD from Jerusalem.' Isaiah 2:3

Jesus will judge from the house of the God of Jacob. His word shall go forth from Jerusalem. Which means Jerusalem must be physically restored before our Lord gathers the nations to see His glory. **(Isa. 2:3, Zech. 6:12-13, Rev. 12:5, Isa. 66:18)**

56. A Remnant Will Return

> Jerusalem is the highest point on earth. The nations will worship Jesus from atop the Mountain of the Lord. The King will teach them His ways and they shall walk in His paths. Just like the prophets foretold.

"And it shall come to pass in that day that the remnant of Israel, and such as have escaped of the house of Jacob, will never again depend on him who defeated them, But will depend on the LORD, the Holy One of Israel, in truth. The remnant will return, the remnant of Jacob, to the Mighty God." Isaiah 10:20-21

After Jerusalem is restored to the highest point on the earth, believers will joyfully return to Zion. (Isa. 2:2-3) The remnant of Jacob will be depending on the Holy One of Israel. Their trust will be in their Mighty God. (Isa. 10:20-21)

"For though your people, O Israel, be as the sand of the sea, a remnant of them will return; the destruction decreed shall overflow with righteousness. For the Lord GOD of hosts will make a determined end in the midst of all the land." Isaiah 10:22-23

"A highway shall be there...called the Highway of Holiness. The unclean shall not pass over it...but the redeemed shall walk there, and the ransomed of the LORD shall return, and come to Zion with singing, with everlasting joy on their heads. They shall obtain joy and gladness, and sorrow and sighing shall flee away." Isaiah 35:8a, 9b, 10

As we studied earlier **(Isa. 10:22-23)**, the redeemed will walk on a Highway of Holiness. **(Isa. 35:8a, 9b, 10)** The ransomed of the Lord will return to Jerusalem with singing and everlasting joy.

'I will bring the one–third through the fire, will refine them as silver is refined, And test them as gold is tested. They will call on My name, And I will answer them I will say, 'This is My people'; And each one will say, "The LORD is my God." Zech. 13:9

The first to return from this remnant may be the redeemed in Azal. **(Zech. 13:9; 14:4-5, Isa. 27:12-13; 35:8-10)** The 144,000 will be the firstfruits saved by God. **(Rev. 7:1-8; 10:1-7; 14:1-4)**

"And it shall come to pass... that the LORD will thresh... you will be gathered one by one, O you children of Israel... They will come, who are about to perish in the land of Assyria, and they who are outcasts in the land of Egypt, and shall worship the LORD in the holy mount at Jerusalem." Isaiah 27:12-13

The Lord will also gather outcasts from Jordan and Egypt. They will come to worship Him atop the Holy Mount at Jerusalem. **(Isa. 27:12-13; 66:18)**

'Therefore thus says the Lord GOD: "I have raised My hand in an oath that surely the nations that are around you shall bear their own shame...Nor will I let you hear the taunts of the nations anymore, nor bear the reproach of the peoples anymore, nor shall you cause your nation to stumble anymore," says the Lord GOD.' Ezekiel 36:7, 15

"Whom have you reproached and blasphemed? Against whom have you raised your voice, And lifted up your eyes on high? Against the Holy One of Israel." Isaiah 37:23

The nations will be ashamed as descendants of Abraham joyfully return to the land promised them. **(Isa. 51:11, Gen. 12:1-3)** Muslims will no longer taunt His children; believers in Jesus. **(Ezek. 36:7, 15)** After seeing the Lord hallowed, they will know not to blaspheme the Holy One of Israel. **(Isa. 37:23)**

"...Behold, this is our God; we have waited for Him, and He will save us. This is the LORD; we have waited for Him; we will be glad and rejoice in His salvation." Isaiah 25:9

'So Christ was offered once to bear the sins of many. To those who eagerly wait for Him He will appear a second time, apart from sin, for salvation.' Hebrews 9:28

At the end of the 70th week of Daniel, a remnant from Israel will eagerly be awaiting His return. The Holy One is coming to forgive them of their sins and bring in everlasting righteousness. **(Dan. 9:24, Isa. 25:9, Heb. 9:28, Rom. 11:25-27)** They will rejoice over their salvation when they see Him in the wilderness. **(Isa. 63:1-6)** Once the wrath of God Almighty is over **(Rev. 19:11-21)**, the ransomed of the Lord will be praising the Holy One of Israel as they return on a highway of holiness. **(Isa. 35:8-10)**

57. I Will Gather All Nations

> The ransomed of the Lord are returning to worship on the Holy Mount. Their trust will forever be in their Mighty God, the Holy One of Israel. Never again will they depend on those who defeated them. Muslim nations will never taunt them again.

'The Lord GOD, who gathers the outcasts of Israel, says, "Yet I will gather to him. Others besides those who are gathered to him." Isaiah 56:8**

"...I will gather all nations and tongues; and they shall come and see My glory." Isaiah 66:18

After gathering the outcasts of Israel back to His Holy Mountain **(Isa. 56:8)**, our Lord will gather Gentiles from the nations. **(Isa. 66:18)**

"...Everyone who is left of all the nations which came against Jerusalem shall go up from year to year to worship the King..." Zechariah 14:16

The Gentiles left among the nations, that came against Jerusalem, will come back to worship the King. **(Zech. 14:16)** Those believing in the gospel will have their names written in the Lamb's Book of Life. **(Rev. 21:24-27)** None of these survivors worshiped the Beast. I ask you, what three wars did they survive? The answer is, the invasion of Jerusalem by the Abomination of Desolation **(Mat. 24:15, Luke 21:20)**, the judgment of Israel's enemies in the Valley of Jehoshaphat **(Joel 3:12-15)**, and the slaughter at the supper of the great God, Armageddon. **(Rev. 16:14-16; 19:17-18)**

58. The Temple Of The Lord

> Their glorious return is a sight to behold. Redeemed Jews are declaring the glory of God to arriving Gentiles. Once their hated enemies, they're coming to worship the King. Those believing in Jesus will have their names written in the Lamb's Book of Life.

"Son of man, describe the temple to the house of Israel that they may be ashamed of their iniquities; and let them measure the pattern." Ezekiel 43:10

Several hundred years before Jesus was born, a prophet saw this temple in a vision. **(Ezek. 40-48)** Ezekiel described the pattern of this future sanctuary to make the children of Israel ashamed of their iniquities. **(Ezekiel 43:10)**

"Even them I will bring to My holy mountain, and make them joyful in My house of prayer...For My house shall be called a house of prayer for all nations." Isaiah 56:7

There will be four temples built atop Mount Moriah.

The first was built by Solomon. **(I Kings 5:3-5; 6:11-14)**
The second was built by the children of Israel. **(Ezra. 6:14)**
The third will be built in the 70th week. **(Rev. 11:2, 2 Thes. 2:3)**
The fourth will be built by the Branch. **(Zech. 6:12-13)**

Isaiah prophesied the temple built by our Lord will be called a house of prayer for all nations. **(Isa. 56:7)**

'And with this the words of the prophets agree... "After this I will return and will rebuild the tabernacle of David, which has fallen down, I will rebuild its ruins, and I will set it up; so that the rest of mankind may seek the LORD..." Acts 15:15-17a

After the Day of the Lord ends, the Tabernacle of David will lay in ruins. **(Acts 15:15-17a)** The restoration of this sanctuary will take place within the forty-five days between Armageddon (1,290 days) and the beginning of Christ's reign over the nations (1,335 days). **(Dan. 12:11-12)** The prophets agree. When our Lord returns He will rule from the Tabernacle of David. **(Zech. 6:12, Ezek. 43:4-7)**

'... "Behold, the Man whose name is the BRANCH. From His place He shall branch out, and He shall build the temple of the LORD." Yes, He shall build the temple of the LORD. He shall bear the glory, and shall sit and rule on His throne; so He shall be a priest on His throne, and the counsel of peace shall be between them both." Zechariah 6:12-13

Who will build the temple of the Lord?
Who shall bear the glory?
Who will rule from His throne?
Who will be the high priest bringing peace?

It can only be the Branch; the Anointed One (Messiah). He will sit as a King and a Priest on His throne. **(Zech. 6:12-13)** Jesus will return to the City of Truth and rebuild the House of the God of Jacob. This is the site Solomon built the House of the Lord. Today it's called the Temple Mount. **(I King. 5:4-5, Mat. 21:13)**

"Come, and let us go up to the mountain of the LORD, to the house of the God of Jacob; He will teach us His ways, and we shall walk in His paths. For out of Zion shall go forth the law, and the word of the LORD from Jerusalem." Isaiah 2:3

The Lord will bring many from the nations to teach them His ways. They shall be His people and He shall be their God. His word will come from the Temple atop the Mountain of the Lord (Jerusalem). **(Isa. 2:3, Ezek. 11:10, Zech. 6:13)**

"Moreover I will make a covenant of peace with them, and it shall be an everlasting covenant with them; I will establish them and multiply them, and I will set My sanctuary in their midst forevermore." Ezekiel 37:26

What will be the everlasting covenant with Israel? Only the Lord can bring everlasting peace. **(Ezek. 37:26; 43:7, Rev. 22:1)** His sanctuary will be set forevermore in the midst of His people. **(Rev. 21:3)** Once He builds the House of God in Jerusalem, believers from the nations will return to worship Him. This stems from the eternal covenant God cut with Abraham and his descendants. **(Gen. 17:2, Gal. 3:29, Rom. 11:25-27)**

"Thus says the Lord: 'I will return to Zion, And dwell in the midst of Jerusalem. Jerusalem shall be called the City of Truth. The Mountain of the Lord of hosts, The Holy Mountain.'" Zechariah 8:3

The Lord will rebuild the tabernacle of David BEFORE ruling over the nations for a thousand years. **(Acts 15:15-17, Zech. 8:3, Rev. 21:9-10)** His throne in the City of Truth will be in the midst of His children for eternity. **(Ezek. 43:2-7, Zech. 6:12-13)**

59. Standing Before The Ancient Of Days

> The restoration of the kingdom of Israel is just days away. Yet the Tabernacle of David lay in ruins. Then it happened. The Branch is rebuilding the Temple atop the Holy Mountain. This house of prayer will be His throne in the midst of His children.

"I was watching in the night visions...One like the Son of Man, coming with the clouds of heaven. He came to the Ancient of Days, and they brought Him near before Him." Daniel 7:13

After building the Temple on earth, the Son of Man will return on the clouds of heaven. **(Zech. 6:12-13, Dan. 7:13)** God the Father will be sitting on His throne when His Son arrives. **(Dan. 7:9, 22)** Jesus is going back to stand before the Ancient of Days.

"Then they will see the Son of Man coming in the clouds with great power and glory." Mark 13:26

The Son of Man will come in the clouds and gather the righteous BEFORE pouring out His wrath on the unrighteous. **(Mat. 24:29-39)**

The Son of Man coming on the clouds of heaven; will stand before the Ancient of Days AFTER His wrath is over. **(Dan. 7:13-14)**

These are two different events our Jesus will fulfill during His Second Coming.

"...Then to Him was given dominion and glory and a kingdom that all peoples, nations, and languages should serve Him. His dominion is an everlasting dominion, which shall not pass away, and His kingdom the one which shall not be destroyed." Daniel 7:14

Jesus is called the Son of Man to emphasize His humanity. **(Mark 9:31; 14:62, Luke 5:24)** He is called the Son of God to emphasize His divinity. **(Luke 1:35, John 10:36)** At this time, the Father will grant His Son dominion over a kingdom. **(Dan. 7:12-14)** This kingdom will consist of peoples and nations who will serve the King of Kings. **(Rev. 19:16; 20:6, 1 Cor. 15:24-28)** Our Lord will rule over a restored earth; an everlasting dominion that will never be destroyed. **(Ezek. 36:35)**

"...You will conceive in your womb and bring forth a Son, and shall call His name JESUS. He will be great, and will be called the Son of the Highest; and the Lord God will give Him the throne of His father David. And He will reign over the house of Jacob forever, and of His kingdom there will be no end." Luke 1:31-33

The Father will grant a kingdom with no end. Gabriel described this incredible event to Mary at our Savior's birth. **(Luke 1:31-33)** The Son of the Highest will be given the throne of David. Our Jesus will rule over the House of Jacob forever. **(Isa. 2:3)**

"Anyone who speaks a word against the Son of Man, it will be forgiven him; but whoever speaks against the Holy Spirit, it will not be forgiven him, either in this age or in the age to come." Matthew 12:32

What is the age to come? It will be the kingdom the Father gives His Son. **(Mat. 12:32, Dan. 7:13-14)** The Holy Spirit will lead many to serve the Lord in Jerusalem. **(Isa. 2:3, Zep. 3:9)** Is there another reason why the Son is returning to heaven? The Son of Man is going back for His bride. Once He is given the kingdom by His Father, the Lamb will descend with His bride inside a new heaven to a new earth. **(Rev. 19:7-9; 21:9-10, 2 Pet. 3:13)**

60. The Reign Of Christ

> Coming back in the clouds, the Son stood before His Father. All of heaven watched the Ancient of Days grant Jesus a kingdom of peoples and nations who will serve Him. The King of Kings will exercise dominion over this kingdom for a thousand years.

'Blessed and holy is he who has part in the first resurrection. Over such the second death has no power, but they shall be priests of God and of Christ and shall reign with Him a thousand years.' Revelation 20:6

The Father will be in heaven when His Son builds the temple of the Lord on earth. Once it's completed, Jesus will ascend to heaven in the clouds. **(Zech. 6:12-13, Dan. 7:13-14)** After receiving a kingdom to rule over from The Ancient of Days, the Lamb and His bride will descend inside a new heaven. They will reign over the nations for a thousand years. **(Rev. 20:6; 21:9-10)**

"...This land that was desolate has become like the Garden of Eden; and the wasted, desolate, and ruined cities are now fortified and inhabited." Ezekiel 36:35

"For behold, I create new heavens and a new earth; and the former shall not be remembered or come to mind. But be glad and rejoice forever in what I create; For behold, I create Jerusalem as a rejoicing and her people a joy...No more shall an infant from there live but a few days, nor an old man who has not fulfilled his days..." Isaiah 65:17-18, 20a

Ezekiel saw a desolate earth being restored like the Garden of Eden. **(Ezek. 36:35)** The ruined cities will be fortified and inhabited with survivors. There will be long life during the reign of Christ. Anyone dying before a hundred years old will be accursed. **(Isa. 65:17-18; 20a; 66:22-24)**

"He shall judge between the nations and rebuke many people; they shall beat their swords into plowshares, and their spears into pruning hooks; Nation shall not lift up sword against nation, neither shall they learn war anymore." Isaiah 2:4

When will our Lord judge between the nations?
When will He rebuke many people?
When will the nation's stop fighting?
When will they not learn war anymore?

Forty-five days after Armageddon, the Lamb of God will begin His rule from the throne of David. **(Dan. 12:11-12, Isa. 9:7)** The city where our Lord was crucified will be the center of the new earth. The above events will take place during His 1,000-year reign. **(Isa. 2:4)**

'... "Behold, the tabernacle of God is with men, and He will dwell with them, and they shall be His people. God Himself will be with them and be their God. And God will wipe away every tear from their eyes; there shall be no more death, nor sorrow, nor crying..."' Revelation 21:3-4

Three groups will be living during the 1,000-year reign of Christ. The first will be the wife of the Lamb. **(Rev. 20:6; 21:9-10)** She will rule within the Tabernacle of God; the Paradise of God. **(Rev. 21:3-4; 2:7)** There will be no more sorrow or pain. Death will be swallowed up in victory. **(1 Cor. 15:54)**

'And the nations of those who are saved shall walk in its light, and the kings of the earth bring their glory and honor into it...' Revelation 21:24

The second group will consist of believers who didn't worship the Beast. They will be saved AFTER the resurrection at the coming of the Son of Man. **(Mat. 24:30-31, Rev. 21:24-27)** These survivors, whose names are written in the Book of Life, will be living on a new earth restored like the Garden Eden. **(Isa. 65:17, Ezek. 36:35)**

'But outside are dogs and sorcerers and sexually immoral and murderers and idolaters, and whoever loves and practices a lie.' Revelation 22:15

The third group will be unsaved survivors. They refused to obey the Beast; nor did they get saved by our Lord. Tragically, sinners will be practicing lies outside the Holy City. This is why the Son must reign a thousand years before putting all enemies under His feet. **(Rev. 21:27; 22:15, 1 Cor. 15:24-27)**

'She bore a male Child...to rule all nations with a rod of iron.' Revelation 12:5

Why will Jesus rule over the nations with a rod of iron during the Millennium? Most think people are a product of their environment. By improving the environment; man will sin less. They believe most will follow God if He were present. These false assertions will be refuted after Satan is released from his prison and deceives the nations like the sand of the sea. **(Rev. 12:5; 20:7-8)**

61. Satan In The Bottomless Pit

> The Ancient of Days granted His Son a kingdom to rule over. The Lamb and His wife are ready to descend to a new earth inside a new heaven. After ruling for a thousand years, the Son of God will deliver this kingdom back to His Father.

'Then I saw an angel coming down from heaven, having the key to the bottomless pit and a great chain in his hand.' Revelation 20:1

What will happen on the first day of the Millennium?
1. The Devil will be bound for a thousand-years. (Rev. 20:1-2)
2. The twelve apostles are given authority to judge. (Rev. 20:4a)
3. The resurrection of martyrs. (Rev. 20:4b)
4. The creation of a new heaven and a new earth. (Rev. 21:1)
5. The return of the Lamb and His Bride. (Rev. 21:9-10)

'He laid hold of the dragon, that serpent of old, who is the Devil and Satan, and bound him for a thousand years.' Revelation 20:2

Who will bind the serpent of old? An angel will come down having a key to the bottomless pit. He will bind Satan with a great chain on the first day of Christ's reign over the nations. (Rev. 20:2; 21:2)

'And he cast him into the bottomless pit, and shut him up, and set a seal on him, so that he should deceive the nations no more till the thousand years were finished. But after these things he must be released for a little while.' Revelation 20:3

Before casting him into the bottomless pit, this angel will put a seal on this foul spirit. This will prevent Satan from deceiving the nations for a thousand years. **(Rev. 20:3-6)**

'Now when the thousand years have expired, Satan will be released from his prison and will go out to deceive the nations which are in the four corners of the earth... to gather them together to battle, whose number is as the sand of the sea. They went up on the breadth of the earth and surrounded the camp of the saints and the beloved city.' Revelation 20:7-9

After a thousand years, Satan will be released from his prison. He will begin by deceiving the nations. The number deceived will be like the sand of the sea. Which means many unsaved people will be on earth when the reign of Christ is finished. Satan's plan is to surround the saints living in the beloved city. **(Rev. 20:7-9)**

"I will no longer talk much with you, for the ruler of this world is coming, and he has nothing in Me." John 14:30

'Those who are sinning rebuke in the presence of all, that the rest also may fear.' 1 Timothy 5:20

In this age, it is heart-wrenching to see so many bought by the blood of Christ being deceived by Satan. **(2 Pet. 2:1, 1 Tim. 4:1)** Today, there are popular teachers deemphasizing the responsibility of a believer. They insist no one should be blamed for sinning. Instead, it is the Devil deceiving them. **(John 14:30)** With Satan bound for a thousand years, no one will be able to offer such a fallacious excuse. **(Rev. 20:1-3)**

62. The Authority To Judge

> The angel bound the Dragon with a chain before casting him into the bottomless pit. This foul spirit will be shut in for a thousand years. Even so, the Devil knows he will be given one more opportunity to deceive the world like the sand of the sea.

"But you shall receive power when the Holy Spirit has come upon you; and you shall be witnesses to Me in Jerusalem, and in all Judea and Samaria, and to the end of the earth." Acts 1:8

The twelve apostles were Peter, John, James, Andrew, Philip, Bartholomew, Matthew, Thomas, James, Thaddaeus, Simon, and Judas Iscariot. **(Mark 3:15-19)** After denying His Lord for thirty pieces of silver, Judas lost his ministry, his apostleship and his salvation. **(Mat. 26:15, Acts 1:16-25)** A faithful apostle named Matthias took his place. **(Acts 1:26)** These faithful men of God preached the kingdom of God to Jews and Gentiles. They were eye witnesses to the end of the earth. **(Acts 1:8)**

'And I saw thrones and they that sat on them, and judgment was committed to them.' Revelation 20:4a

"...Assuredly I say to you...when the Son of Man sits on the throne of His glory, you who have followed Me will also sit on twelve thrones, judging the twelve tribes of Israel." Matthew 19:28

Who will judge the twelve tribes of Israel? On the first day of His 1,000-year reign, the Son will fulfill this promise. He will grant the first preachers of Christianity the authority to judge the twelve tribes of Israel. From the throne of His glory, Jesus will give a kingdom to the apostles who followed Him in His trials. **(Rev. 20:6, Mat. 19:28, Luke 22:28-30)**

"But you are those who have continued with Me in My trials. And I bestow upon you a kingdom, just as My Father bestowed one upon Me." Luke 22:28-29

The restoration of all things is a restored earth with Jerusalem at its highest point. **(Acts 3:21, Isa. 2:1-4)** This restoration will begin when the Messiah physically returns for the salvation of Israel on the Day of Atonement. **(Dan. 9:24, Rev. 10:7)** Seventy-five days later, the same day Satan is bound (1,260-1,335 days), the twelve apostles will be given a kingdom to judge. **(Dan. 12:12, Rev. 20:1-2, Luke 22:28-29, Rev. 20:4a)**

63. The Resurrection Of Martyrs

> Oozing with excitement, a host of angels stood to attention. The twelve apostles, whose names are written on the foundations of the holy city, knelt before His throne. His wife erupted in praise after the Son bestowed upon them a kingdom to judge.

'...Then I saw the souls of those who had been beheaded for their witness to Jesus and for the word of God, who had not worshiped the beast or his image, and had not received his mark on their foreheads or on their hands...' Revelation 20:4a

The next event will be the resurrection of souls beheaded for their witness of Jesus and the word of God. These saints refused to worship the Beast or receive his mark. **(Rev. 20:4a)**

'...And they lived and reigned with Christ for a thousand years.' Revelation 20:4b

There will be believers in heaven after the Lamb opens the fifth seal. **(Rev. 6:9-11)** These martyrs killed by the Beast are told to wait until the number of their brethren is completed. Amazingly enough, they won't be raised till the first day of Christ's 1,000-year reign. **(Rev. 20:4, 6)** Like those saved during the millennium, they will receive their glorified bodies after the coming of the Son of Man, after the judgment seat of Christ, and after the marriage of the Lamb. **(Rev. 7:9-17; 11:18; 19:7)** The resurrection of the dead in Christ **(1 Thes. 4:15-16)** and the resurrection of those martyred by the Beast **(Rev. 20:4)** will take place at different times; yet both are part of the first resurrection. **(Rev. 20:5)**

'But the rest of the dead did not live again until the thousand years were finished. This is the first resurrection.' Revelation 20:5

The wicked dead won't live again until the 1,000-year reign of Christ is finished. **(Rev. 20:5)** Once Satan is cast into the lake of fire, they will be resurrected out of Hades, stand before the Great White Throne, and be judged by Jesus. **(Rev. 20:7-15)**

'Blessed and holy is he who has part in the first resurrection. Over such the second death has no power, but they shall be priests of God and of Christ and shall reign with Him a thousand years.' Revelation 20:6

Everyone martyred by the Beast will join the Bride inside the New Jerusalem and become priests of God and of Christ. **(Rev. 20:6; 21:9-10)** Every believer participating in the first resurrection will not be hurt by the second death. The second death is separation from God in the lake of fire for eternity. **(Rev. 20:14-15)**

'But now Christ is risen from the dead, and has become the firstfruits of those who have fallen asleep. For since by man came death, by Man also came the resurrection of the dead.' 1 Corinthians 15:20-21

The first resurrection has four phases. **(1 Cor. 15:20-21, 22-23, Rev. 20:4; 21:24)** Adam's sin brought spiritual and physical death. **(Gen. 3:14-19)** This is why God provided a way for His creation to become spiritually alive again. Our Father sent His Son to die for our sins and defeat death. **(1 Cor. 15:3, Rom. 5:12-21)** Jesus was the first to rise from the dead and live forevermore. The Christ is the firstfruits of the first resurrection. **(1 Cor. 15:20-21)**

'For as in Adam all die, even so in Christ all shall be made alive. But each one in his own order: Christ the firstfruits, afterward those who are Christ's at His coming...' 1 Corinthians 15:22-23

The second phase is the resurrection of the dead in Christ and the translation of alive believers. **(1 Thes. 4:16-17, Mark 13:26-27)** Old and New Testament believers will be made alive at His Second Coming. **(1 Cor. 15:22-23, 50-52)**

'... And they lived and reigned with Christ for a thousand years.' Revelation 20:4b

The third phase is those martyred by the Beast. During the Great Tribulation, many will suffer death for the sake of His name. They will be raised incorruptible and reign with Christ on the first day of His thousand-year reign. **(Rev. 12:11; 20:4b; 21:9-10)**

'And the nations of those who are saved shall walk in its light, and the kings of the earth bring their glory and honor into it.' Revelation 21:24

There will be believers living among the nations when the Lamb and His bride descend within the Holy Jerusalem. **(Rev. 21:9-10)** During His 1,000-year reign, they will be able to enter through the gates of the holy city. **(Rev. 22:14)** Every believer living on a new earth will eventually join His wife. **(Rev. 22:1-5)** All in Christ shall be made spiritually alive for eternity. **(1 Cor. 15:22)** Blessed are those the second death has no power over. **(Rev. 2:11)** This will be the final phase of the first resurrection. **(Rev. 21:24-27)**

64. A New Heaven And A New Earth

> Mocked as crazy fanatics, their betrayal by family and friends was a heartbreak. No one protested when the False Prophet had them killed. The honoring of these resurrected saints is before them. They will reign with Christ as the priests of God.

'Then He who sat on the throne said, "Behold, I make all things new." And He said to me, "Write, for these words are true and faithful." Revelation 21:5**

Both heaven and earth will melt with fervent heat. **(2 Pet. 3:10)** Our Lord will announce He has made all things new. The Alpha and the Omega will declare it is done. **(Rev. 1:11; 21:5-6)**

"For behold, I create new heavens and a new earth; and the former shall not be remembered or come to mind." Isaiah 65:17

'Nevertheless we, according to His promise, look for new heavens and a new earth in which righteousness dwells.' 2 Peter 3:13

'Now I saw a new heaven and a new earth, for the first heaven and the first earth had passed away...' Revelation 21:1

Isaiah, Peter, and John each saw a new heaven and a new earth. **(Isa. 65:17, 2 Pet. 3:13, Rev. 21:1)** Passing away means to pass from one form to another. A desolate earth will undergo a glorious restoration. Earth will abide forever. **(Ezek. 36:35, Ecc.1:4)**

"This land that was desolate has become like the Garden of Eden; and the wasted, desolate, and ruined cities are now fortified and inhabited." Ezekiel 36:35

The earth will burn up during the Day of the Lord. **(2 Pet. 3:10-12, Isa. 13:9-11)** Even so, God is going to transform this desolate earth into a Garden of Eden. Wasted cities ruined by hundred-pound hailstones will be fortified and inhabited. **(Ezek. 36:35, Rev. 16:20-21)** Saved and unsaved survivors will witness a demolished earth being restored. **(Rev. 21:24-27)**

"Then say to them, 'Thus says the Lord GOD: "Surely I will take the children of Israel from among the nations, wherever they have gone, and will gather them from every side and bring them into their own land." Ezekiel 37:21

"...I will gather all nations and tongues; and they shall come and see My glory." Isaiah 66:18

After the redeemed safely return to Jerusalem, our Lord will gather Gentiles from all the nations to see His glory. **(Ezek. 37:21, Isa. 66:18)**

"Behold, the tabernacle of God is with men, and He will dwell with them, and they shall be His people. God Himself will be with them and be their God." Revelation 21:3

'The city is laid out as a square...And he measured the city with the reed: twelve thousand furlongs. Its length, breadth, and height are equal. Then he measured its wall: one hundred and forty-four cubits...' Revelation 21:16-17

The Lord will wipe away every tear from the saints dwelling inside the tabernacle of God. **(Rev. 21:3)** There will be no more sorrow or death. Jesus calls this Holy City His Father's house. Inside are mansions He promised His disciples. His wife will dwell for eternity within the Holy Jerusalem. **(John 14:1-4, Rev. 21:9-10)** John wrote down the dimensions. The length, breadth, and height of the four-square city will be 1,500 miles. Its walls will be 200 feet high. **(Rev. 21:16-17, Mic. 4:1)**

'Many people shall come and say, "Come, and let us go up to the mountain of the LORD, To the house of the God of Jacob; He will teach us His ways, And we shall walk in His paths." For out of Zion shall go forth the law, And the word of the LORD from Jerusalem.' Isaiah 2:3

The New Jerusalem will join the house of the God of Jacob built upon the mountain of the Lord. **(Rev. 21:9-10)** This house of prayer is the physical temple the Branch will build. **(Zech. 6:12, Ezek. 43:1-7)** People from the nations will flow to this temple in Jerusalem to hear the word of the Lord. **(Isa. 2:1-4)**

'But now they desire a better, that is, a heavenly country. Therefore, God is not ashamed to be called their God, for He has prepared a city for them.' Hebrews 11:16

"He who overcomes, I will make him a pillar in the temple of My God, and he shall go out no more. I will write on him the name of My God and the name of the city of My God, the New Jerusalem, which comes down out of heaven from My God. And I will write on him My new name." Revelation 3:12

Paul spoke of those in the faith seeking a better homeland. They were pilgrims on this earth. They lived their lives with an eye on a heavenly country. God is not ashamed to be called their God. **(Heb. 11:16)** So, why is the promise of the New Jerusalem coming down from heaven rarely taught today? **(Rev. 3:12; 21:2)**

65. The Lamb And His Bride

> A desolate earth is being miraculously transformed. Ruined cities are being fortified and inhabited. At the same time, a new heaven has replaced the old heaven that was dissolved by fire. The restoration of all things is near.

'... **"Come, I will show you the bride, the Lamb's wife. And he carried me away in the Spirit to a great and high mountain, and showed me the great city, the holy Jerusalem, descending out of heaven from God..." Revelation 21:9-10**

On the first day of their 1,000-year reign over the nations **(Rev. 20:6)**, the Lamb and His bride will descend to earth within the great city, the Holy Jerusalem. **(Rev 21:2, 9-10)**

'And the glory of the LORD came into the temple by way of the gate which faces toward the east. The Spirit lifted me up and brought me into the inner court; and behold, the glory of the LORD filled the temple.' Ezekiel 43:4-5

Hanukkah means 'dedication'. The Feast of Dedication is a celebration of the rededication of the temple desecrated by the Gentiles. During this ceremony, the purifying of the altar by fire is patterned after the glory of the Lord filling the first temple. **(2 Chr. 5:3; 7:1)** Jesus personally participated in this Feast of Dedication. **(John 10:22-30)** Every year, there are seventy-five days between the Day of Atonement (1,260 days) and Hanukkah (1,335 days). **(Rev. 10:1-7, Dan. 12:12)** Believers dwelling on a new earth will be blessed as they wait for the Lamb of God to return during this Feast of Lights. **(Rev. 21:9-10)** His Second Coming will end with a glorious dedication of the rebuilt Tabernacle of David. **(Zech. 6:12, Acts 15:15-17)** Our Lord will fill this sanctuary with His Shekinah glory. **(Ezek. 43:4-5)**

'Then he said to me, "Write: Blessed are those who are called to the marriage supper of the Lamb!" Revelation 19:9

The celebration of the marriage supper will begin after the Lamb and His wife return to a new earth. **(Rev. 19:7; 20:6; 21:9-10)** Those written in the Lamb's Book of Life will enter through the gates of the Holy City and celebrate the marriage supper of the Lamb. **(Rev. 19:9; 21:24-27; 22:14)**

'Consider what I say, and may the Lord give you understanding in all things.' 2 Timothy 2:7

The Second Coming will begin during the Feast of Trumpets (Rosh Hashanah). At the last trump, the Son of Man will send forth His angels to gather believers to heaven before pouring out His wrath on the wicked. **(1 Cor 15:52, Mat. 24:29-39)**

At the end of the second half of 70th week of Daniel (1,260 days), the Holy One will physically return on the Day of Atonement (Yom Kippur). **(Dan. 9:24, Rom. 11:25-27, Rev. 10:1-7)**

Five days later, during the Feast of Tabernacles (Sukkot), Jesus will finish the mystery of God; the salvation of Israel. **(Rev. 14:1-4)**

The next day, Jesus will split the Mount of Olives and hide His redeemed remnant in Azal from the seven bowl judgments. Jesus will then return to heaven for the judgment seat of Christ followed by His marriage to His bride. **(Rev. 11:15; 19:7)**

Thirty days after the Day of Atonement (1,290 days), the Word of God will appear at the great day of God Almighty, Armageddon. Jesus will cast the two beasts into the lake of fire and kill their followers. **(Dan 12:11, Rev. 16:14-16; 19:11-21)**

After rebuilding the temple of God, the Son of Man will return to heaven and stand before the Ancient of Days for two reasons. The Father will grant His Son a kingdom to rule. And Jesus is going back to get His bride. **(Dan. 7:13)**

His Second Coming will end on the first day of their 1,000-year reign over the nations (1,335 days). **(Rev. 20:6; 21:9-11, Dan. 12:12)** The survivors living on a new earth will watch the Lamb of God and His bride descend within a new heaven! **(Rev. 21:24-27)**

'Then I, John, saw the holy city, New Jerusalem, coming down out of heaven from God, prepared as a bride adorned for her husband.' Revelation 21:1-2

It's important to understand the events John wrote down in his letter do not take place in chronological order. It is true, the seven seals **(Rev. 6:1-17; 8:1)**, the seven trumpets **(Rev. 8:7-13; 9:1-21; 11:15)** and the seven bowls **(Rev.16:1-21)** will take place one right after the other. Yet, there are other events in his vision that flashback to an earlier time. For example, most scholars teach Satan must be released from his 1,000-year prison sentence BEFORE the New Jerusalem descends to a new earth. Why is this interpretation not possible?

'Now when the thousand years have expired, Satan will be released from his prison.' Revelation 20:7

'... "Come, I will show you the bride, the Lamb's wife." And he carried me away in the Spirit to a great and high mountain, and showed me the great city, the holy Jerusalem, descending out of heaven from God.' Revelation 21:9b-10

I ask you, how can the Lamb and His bride rule for a thousand years if they return after the Millennium (1,000 years) is over?

'Blessed are those who do His commandments, that they may have the right to the tree of life, and may enter through the gates into the city.' Revelation 22:14

How can anyone enter through the gates of the city if the New Jerusalem doesn't descend until after the Millennium is over?

'She bore a male Child who was to rule all nations with a rod of iron. And her Child was caught up to God and His throne.' Revelation 12:5

Now we know mankind will be devoured by fire at the end of the 1,000 years. **(Rev. 20:9)** So how can Jesus rule with an iron hand if He returns after the Millennium is over? **(Rev. 12:5)**

As you can see, not all events in the Revelation of Jesus Christ take place in order. Scripture clearly teaches the Lamb and His wife will rule at the beginning of the 1,000 years; not at the end. **(Ezek. 36:35, Rev. 21:2-10, Isa. 65:17-20)**

66. The Throne Of God

> The survivors watched as the Lamb and His wife descended within the Holy Jerusalem. Believers cheered as the four-square city joined the Mountain of the Lord. Entering the eastern gate, Jesus filled the Temple with His Shekinah glory.

'Also she had a great and high wall with twelve gates, and twelve angels at the gates, and names written on them, which are the names of the twelve tribes of the children of Israel...' Revelation 21:12

"For as the new heavens and the new earth Which I will make shall remain before Me," says the LORD, "So shall your descendants and your name remain." Isaiah 66:22

John saw a great wall of the New Jerusalem having twelve gates. The names of the twelve tribes of Israel are written on these gates. **(Rev. 21:12; 7:4-8)** This is an eternal remembrance of how powerfully God used the children of Israel. Israel and her descendants will remain forever. **(Isa. 66:22)**

'But I saw no temple in it, for the Lord God Almighty and the Lamb are its temple. The city had no need of the sun or of the moon to shine in it for the glory of God illuminated it. The Lamb is its light.' Revelation 21:22-23

Why no temple in the Holy City? It's because the Lord God Almighty and the Lamb are its temple. The Lamb is its light. Light from the sun, moon, and stars are absent because the glory of God is illuminating this four-square city. **(Rev. 21:22-23)**

'Blessed are those who do His commandments, that they may have the right to the tree of life, and may enter through the gates into the city.' Revelation 22:14

'And the nations of those who are saved shall walk in its light, and the kings of the earth bring their glory and honor into it...But there shall by no means enter it anything that defiles, or causes an abomination or a lie, but only those who are written in the Lamb's Book of Life.' Revelation 21:24, 27

Who will bring honor into the Holy City? (**Rev. 22:14**) During the thousand-year reign of Christ, both saved and unsaved people will be living on a new earth. Those written in the Lamb's Book of Life may pass through the gates of the city. The wicked will never be allowed to enter. (**Rev. 21:24, 27**)

'And it shall come to pass that everyone who is left of all the nations which came against Jerusalem shall go up from year to year to worship the King, the LORD of hosts, and to keep the Feast of Tabernacles.' Zechariah 14:16

Those left from the nations will worship the Lord of hosts. Each year during the reign of Christ, they will celebrate the Feast of Tabernacles. Anyone refusing to come will receive no rain. (**Zech. 14:16-17**)

'And he showed me a pure river of water of life, clear as crystal, proceeding from the throne of God and of the Lamb. In the middle of its street, and on either side of the river, was the tree of life, which bore twelve fruits, each tree yielding its fruit every month. The leaves of the tree were for the healing of the nations.' Revelation 22:1-2

Within the Holy City, a river of life will proceed from the throne of God. Planted on both sides of the river is the tree of life. During Christ's reign, there will people on earth suffering sickness and physical death. **(Isa. 65:20, Rev. 20:7-9)** This is why the leaves from the tree of life will be used for their healing. **(Rev. 22:1-2)**

'And there shall be no more curse, but the throne of God and of the Lamb shall be in it, and His servants shall serve Him. They shall see His face, and His name shall be on their foreheads.' Revelation 22:3-4

There will be no curses within the Holy City. Believers will see His face. His name will be on their foreheads. **(Rev. 22:3-4)** They will abide with Him forever and ever. **(Rev. 21:3)**

'Afterward he brought me to the gate, the gate that faces toward the east. And behold, the glory of the God of Israel came from the way of the east. His voice was like the sound of many waters; and the earth shone with His glory.' Ezekiel 43:1-2

This is the temple Ezekiel saw in his vision. The Branch will build the temple of the Lord before returning with His wife. **(Zech. 6:12-13)** His voice will be like the sound of many waters. His glory will shine upon the new earth. **(Ezek. 43:1-2)**

'And the glory of the LORD came into the temple by way of the gate which faces toward the east. The Spirit lifted me up and brought me into the inner court; and behold, the glory of the LORD filled the temple.' Ezekiel 43:4-5

Our Lord will enter the eastern gate of the temple on the first day of His thousand-year reign. **(Ezek. 43:4-5)** He will rule from His physical throne. **(Dan. 7:13-14)** The entire area surrounding the temple is holy. Jesus will forever dwell in the House of God of Jacob. **(Isa. 2:2-3)**

'And he showed me a pure river of water of life, clear as crystal, proceeding from the throne of God and of the Lamb.' Revelation 22:1

John saw the Lamb and the throne of God inside the holy city. **(Rev. 22:1)** Ezekiel saw the Lord dwelling forever inside a physical temple on earth. So how can Jesus rule within the heavenly city and the physical temple in Jerusalem at the same time? Let's compare passages and see how.

John saw the holy city illuminated by God's glory.
Zechariah saw the Lord bearing the glory within the temple.
(Rev. 21:23-24, Zech. 6:13)

John saw precious stones adorned on the walls of the holy city.
Isaiah saw precious stones on the walls of the temple.
(Rev. 21:18-19, Isa. 54:11-12)

John saw water proceeding from the throne of God.
Joel saw water flowing from the House of the Lord.
(Rev. 22:1, Joel 3:18)

John saw leaves from the tree of life being used for healing.
Ezekiel saw the leaves will be used as medicine for healing.
(Rev. 22:2, Ezek. 47:12)

John saw believers bringing glory into the holy city.
Ezekiel saw the children of Israel entering the sanctuary.
(Rev. 21:24-26, Ezek. 44:9)

John saw the throne of God inside the holy city.
Ezekiel saw His throne in the midst of His children forever.
(Rev. 21:1, Ezek. 43:7)

After comparing scriptures, it's clear the temple in Jerusalem will become the throne of God within the Holy Jerusalem!

67. Satan Released To Deceive

> The saints from the nations are bringing glory and honor into the Holy Jerusalem. Passing through the open gates was much more than they ever imagined. When they saw the Father and His Son they dropped to their knees in praise and worship.

'Pray for the peace of Jerusalem: May they prosper who love you...Because of the house of the LORD our God I will seek your good.' Psalm 122:6, 9

When we pray for the peace of Jerusalem **(Psa. 122:6-9)**, we are actually praying for Christ's future reign over the nations. **(Rev. 20:6)** From the House of the Lord, Jesus will judge and rebuke many people. **(Mic. 4:3, Rev. 12:5)** There will be no more war. The result will be a worldwide peace. **(Isa. 2:1-4)**

'Now when the thousand years have expired, Satan will be released from his prison and will go out to deceive the nations which are in the four corners of the earth... to gather them together to battle, whose number is as the sand of the sea.' Revelation 20:7-8

Satan will be released from the bottomless pit after a thousand years of torment. **(Rev. 20:1-3)** Not experiencing any spiritual warfare for a millennium, the wicked will easily trust in the power from this foul spirit. His plan is to deceive them into attacking the camp of the saints. **(Rev. 20:7-9)**

'They went up on the breadth of the earth and surrounded the camp of the saints and the beloved city. And fire came down from God out of heaven and devoured them.' Revelation 20:9

How will mankind be destroyed? We aren't told how long it will take Satan to gather the wicked against the saints. Once they surround Jerusalem, fire will come down from God and devour them. **(Rev. 20:9)** This will destroy the final rebellion of man. No one will be left alive. This fire will not affect the new earth. Instead, it will destroy the enemies of Christ. **(1 Cor. 15:25)**

'And the Spirit and the bride say, "Come." And let him who hears say, "Come. And let him who thirsts come. Whoever desires, let him take the water of life freely." Revelation 22:17

It will be a different story for the saved among the nations. **(Rev. 21:24-27)** The Spirit and the bride will invite them to come inside the Holy City and drink the water of eternal life. **(Rev. 22:17)** They will enter through the gates and join their brothers and sisters in Christ. **(Rev. 21:24-26; 22:14)** They will receive their glorified bodies and walk in the light of the New Jerusalem before the thousand-year reign of Christ ends. **(Rev. 20:6; 21:24)**

68. Tormented Forever

> No one noticed his release from the bottomless pit. Like the sand of the sea, Satan's deception reached the four corners of earth. Once his armies surrounded the camp of the saints, fire from God ended their rebellion. The human race is no more.

'Then shall he say... "Depart from me, ye cursed, into everlasting fire, prepared for the Devil and his angels." Matthew 25:41

Everlasting fire was originally prepared for the Devil and his angels. **(Mat. 25:41)** It will be enlarged for the wicked. **(Rev. 20:11-15)**

'The devil, who deceived them, was cast into the lake of fire and brimstone where the beast and the false prophet are. And they will be tormented day and night forever and ever.' Revelation 20:10

What will be the fate of the Devil? At the supper of the great God, the Beast and the False Prophet will be cast alive into the lake of fire. **(Rev. 19:11-21)** The Devil will join these evil deceivers after mankind is devoured by fire. **(Rev. 19:11-21; 20:9-10)**

'...And they will be tormented day and night forever and ever.' Revelation 20:10b

Another doctrine of demons making inroads into the church is the lie the lake of fire is symbolic. Many are convinced a loving God is not capable of tormenting anyone. Instead, they teach the wicked will simply be annihilated. This is another example of denying what God has declared. **(Rev. 14:10)** How do we know the Beast and the False Prophet will not be annihilated after being cast into the lake of fire? **(Rev. 19:20)** After a thousand years, the Devil will join them in their eternal suffering. **(Rev. 20:10-15)**

'... "If anyone worships the beast and his image, and receives his mark on his forehead or on his hand, he himself shall also drink of the wine of the wrath of God..." Revelation 14:9-10

Anyone denying the Lord by worshiping the Beast, his image, or receiving his mark will be tormented in fire and brimstone. They will drink the wine of the wrath of God in the presence of holy angels and the Lamb. The smoke of their torment will ascend forever. There will never be any rest from this fire. **(Rev. 14:9-11)**

"If your hand or foot causes you to sin, cut it off and cast it from you. It is better for you to enter into life lame or maimed, rather than having two hands or two feet, to be cast into the everlasting fire." Matthew 18:8

"And these will go away into everlasting punishment, but the righteous into eternal life." Matthew 25:46

Is sharing the eternal fate of the wicked an act of love? Have you ever thought about the unbearable pain of everlasting fire? No amount of screaming, pleading, or begging will change anything. There is no exit from the lake of fire. **(Mat. 18:8, Rev. 20:15)** Their souls will never cease to exist. How can we not warn the wicked of everlasting punishment? **(Mat. 25:46)** The world believes this is a scare tactic. Nothing could be further from the truth.

69. A Great White Throne

> Passing through the flames Satan saw them groveling for relief. They couldn't speak. Their agony is excruciating. The judgment of this evil trilogy is final. The Devil, the Beast, and the False Prophet will be tormented in the Lake of Fire for eternity.

"For the Father judges no one, but has committed all judgment to the Son, that all should honor the Son just as they honor the Father. He who does not honor the Son does not honor the Father who sent Him." John 5:22-23

Our Father has committed all judgment to His Son. Anyone not honoring the Son, is not honoring His Father who sent Him. **(John 5:22-23)** The saints enduring with Him will reign with Him. Those choosing to deny the Son, Jesus will deny. **(2 Tim. 2:12)**

'Then I saw a great white throne and Him who sat on it, from whose face the earth and the heaven fled away. And there was found no place for them. And I saw the dead, small and great, standing before God, and books were opened...And the dead were judged according to their works, by the things which were written in the books. The sea gave up the dead who were in it, and Death and Hades delivered up the dead who were in them. And they were judged, each one according to his works.' Revelation 20:11-13

The Son of God will judge the wicked from a Great White Throne between heaven and earth. Those never saved will be resurrected out of Hades and be judged according to their works written in the books. Some will be punished more than others. This proves there will be different degrees of torment. **(Rev. 20:11-13)**

'...Anyone not found written in the Book of Life was cast into the lake of fire.' Revelation 20:15

The Book of Life will also be opened at the Great White Throne. It doesn't matter how unfair your life was, how many people you helped, or what you achieved. If your name is not written in this book you will suffer in the lake of fire for eternity. **(Rev. 20:15)**

'...He shall be tormented with fire and brimstone in the presence of the holy angels and in the presence of the Lamb.' Revelation 14:10

Anyone who worships the Beast or receives his mark will be tormented in fire and brimstone in the presence of the Lamb and His holy angels. **(Rev. 14:10)**

'Then Death and Hades were cast into the lake of fire. This is the second death.' Revelation 20:14

When will physical Death and Hades cease? **(Rev. 1:18)** The wicked dead are presently suffering in Hades (hell fire). After they're cast into the lake of fire at the Great White Throne, Death and Hades will join them. **(Rev. 20:11-15)** Both are temporary. **(1 Cor. 15:55-57)** There is a time to be born and a time to die. **(Ecc. 3:2)** Neither will ever happen again. **(Rev. 20:14)**

'But why do you judge your brother? Or why do you show contempt for your brother? For we shall all stand before the judgment seat of Christ...So then each of us shall give account of himself to God.' **Romans 14:10, 12**

After the sounding of the seventh trumpet **(Rev. 11:15-18**, the Son will return to heaven to preside over the **JUDGMENT SEAT OF CHRIST.** **(2 Cor 5:10-11, Rom. 14:10, 12)** Every saint will give an account of himself. All works will be tested by fire. Works done for the glory of God will be rewarded. Works of the flesh will burn up. **(1 Cor. 3:11-15)**

'Then I saw a great white throne and Him who sat on it, from whose face the earth and the heaven fled away. And there was found no place for them.' **Revelation 20:11**

After the 1,000-year reign of Christ is completed, the dead in Hades will stand before the **GREAT WHITE THRONE**. At this final judgment, the wicked will be cast into the eternal lake of fire. **(Rev. 20:7-15, Mat. 25:41)**

How will these two events differ?
The Judgment Seat of Christ is for the saved. **(Rev. 11:18)**
The Great White Throne is for the unsaved. **(Rev. 20:11-15)**

70. Then Comes The End

> The wicked stood before His great white throne. No one was found in the Book of Life. After being judged for their works, Death and Hades were cast into the lake of fire. It wasn't long before they too suffered the second death.

'THEN COMES THE END, when He delivers the kingdom to God the Father, when He puts an end to all rule and all authority and power. For He must reign till He has put all enemies under His feet.' 1 Corinthians 15:24-25

The end will come when the Son puts an end to all rule, authority, and power. **(1 Cor. 15:24-25)** After Satan is released from his prison, this evil spirit will gather the wicked against the camp of the saints. **(Rev. 20:8-9)** During this final rebellion, God will devour the entire human race with fire. Then Satan will be cast into the lake of fire. **(Rev. 20:10)** At the great White Throne Judgment, Death, Hades, and the wicked dead will also be cast into the lake of fire. **(Rev. 20:11-15)** After putting all enemies under His feet, the Son will deliver the kingdom back to His Father. **(Dan. 7:13-14)**

'The last enemy that will be destroyed is death...' 1 Corinthians 15:26

The last enemy of God is physical death. Eternity will begin once Death is cast into the lake of fire. How so? No one will ever die again. **(1 Cor. 15:26, Rev. 20:14)**

'For there are three that bear witness in heaven: the Father, the Word, and the Holy Spirit; and these three are one.' 1 John 5:7

The triune nature of God is the cornerstone of the doctrine of Christ. The Father, the Word, and the Holy Spirit have always existed as one God. There is One God consisting of three persons. **(1 John 5:7, Gen. 1:26)**

The Father is the Ancient of Days. **(Dan. 7:13-14)**
The Son is the Word of God. **(John 1:1-14)**
The Holy Spirit is the Spirit of God. **(Mat. 12:28)**

'Now when all things are made subject to Him, then the Son Himself will also be subject to Him who put all things under Him, that God may be all in all.' 1 Corinthians 15:28

When will God become all in all? After destroying all His enemies, the Son will subject Himself to His Father. **(Dan. 7:13-14, 1 Cor. 15:24-28)** He will do this so the Father, the Son, and the Holy Spirit may be all in all. **(1 John 5:7, Mat. 28:18-19, 1 Cor. 15:24-28)** Surely, this glorious event will be honored throughout eternity!

A Final Exhortation

> Jesus must reign until He puts all enemies under His feet. Everyone cheered as His last enemy, Death, was cast into the lake of fire. After subjecting Himself to His Father; the Son delivered the Kingdom back so God may be all in all.

"But hold fast what you have till I come. And he who overcomes, and keeps My works until the end, to him I will give power over the nations." Revelation 2:25-26

To keep His works until the end, one must continually abide in the doctrine of Christ. For those who hold fast and overcome, Jesus will give power over the nations. It will be a different fate for believers taking away from The Revelation of Jesus Christ.

"And if anyone takes away from the words of the book of this prophecy, God shall take away his part from the Book of Life, from the holy city, and from the things which are written in this book." Revelation 22:19

For those who do, God will take away their part in the Book of Life and the Holy City. Within this final exhortation, for the sake of the church, I feel led to expose four deceptions taking away from the most prophetic book in the Bible.

1. The gifts of the Spirit have ceased. **(Rev. 2:11)**
2. The Beast will never war against the saints. **(Rev. 13:7)**
3. The elect cannot lose their crowns. **(Rev. 3:11)**
4. The Second Coming is a single visit. **(Rev. 1:7; 21:9-10)**

'...He breathed on them, and said to them, "Receive the Holy Spirit." John 20:22

The time was March 22nd, 1975. The place, a cozy town off the coast of California called Santa Barbara. It was a warm Saturday night with a light breeze. My friends were witnessing to me in the living room of their condominium. They patiently shared the gospel and His promise to come back. Our talk lasted three hours but it felt like twenty minutes. After they finished, I got down on my knees and asked Jesus to forgive me of my sins and be my Lord and Savior. I'll never forget the peace I felt that night after receiving the Holy Spirit.

'And these signs will follow those who believe: In My name they will cast out demons; they will speak with new tongues.' Mark 16:17

A year later, I was studying the Book of Acts. The evening Jesus rose from the dead, He breathed on His disciples and they received the Holy Spirit. Fifty days later, during the Feast of Weeks (Pentecost), these same men were filled with the Holy Spirit and spoke in tongues. I discovered these are two different experiences. One must receive the indwelling of the Spirit before being baptized in the Spirit. That night I prayed and received the promise of the Father. I could really feel the presence of God after speaking in tongues for the first time. The next morning, I eagerly shared with my Sunday school class how I received the gift of speaking in tongues. It was like a bomb going off. Welcome to spiritual warfare 101. A few days later I received a phone call from our youth pastor. When we met in his office he explained why the gifts of the Spirit ceased in the first century. He made it clear speaking in tongues is demonic. He forbid me to mention I speak in tongues. For a baby Christian, it was challenging to say the least. The only way to be free from this spirit of control was to obey the Holy Spirit. My decision to leave helped me defeat the fear of man later in my life.

"He who has an ear, let him hear what the Spirit says to the churches." Revelation 2:29

We often hear pastors teach the Spirit only speaks through the scriptures. What is the fruit of this deception? Tragically, those no longer hearing His voice are being deceived by the enemy. Below are three instances when the Spirit of God not only spoke to me (not in an audible voice); He told me what to do.

'Therefore, as the Holy Spirit says: "Today, if you will hear His voice." Hebrews 3:7

I remember like it was yesterday. That night I fell asleep while driving up a steep mountain road! At the same time, a drunk driver sped over the top of the hill in his truck. I suddenly woke up and heard in my mind turn right. After I turned, his truck crushed the passenger door behind me. My demolished car had to be carted away. If I hadn't obeyed I would have been killed. Who spoke this word of knowledge? Was it my imagination, a demon or the Holy Spirit?

A friend of mine was a first-time author. Jim was excited about his invitation to attend the National Christian Book Seller's Convention. A voice in my mind said Jim should be ready to share the gospel with Robert Schuller. This famous pastor believes everyone will go to heaven. I warned Jim not to be deceived. The dinner for the authors was the first night. The writer seated next to Jim was distant and into himself. After a few minutes, Robert Schuller left! Who spoke this word of knowledge? Was it my imagination, a demon or the Holy Spirit?

During my time at seminary, I was preparing to take a test in Biblical Literature. Just minutes before, I heard in my mind page 151. I turned to this page and studied the Canaanite religion. The first question on the exam was explain the relationship between Judaism and the Canaanite religion. Who spoke this word of knowledge? Was it my imagination, a demon, or the Holy Spirit?

"He who has an ear, let him hear what the Spirit says to the churches. He who overcomes shall not be hurt by the second death." Revelation 2:11

In this late hour, those listening to the voice of the Spirit are being taught what to say. But, Paul, many believe this isn't possible. My friends, the barometer of one's faithfulness is hearing and obeying the Holy Spirit. Those denying this are doing neither.

This is why anyone believing the gifts of the Spirit has ceased is taking away from The Revelation of Jesus Christ.

'And I saw something like a sea of glass mingled with fire, and those who have the victory over the beast, over his image and over his mark and over the number of his name, standing on the sea of glass, having harps of God.' Revelation 15:2

What deceptive smokescreen is taking away from the timing of the Second Coming? The Son of Man won't be gathering His elect from the wrath to come, before, in the middle, or at the end of the 70th Week of Daniel. Think of the countless hours teachers have vainly tried to prove a pre-tribulation, mid-tribulation, post-tribulation timing of His Coming. These interpretations aren't in the scriptures; nor are they from the Holy Spirit. So, what is our Lord really saying? The saints getting the victory over the Beast will know their gathering by angels is near when they see the sun, the moon, and the stars lose their light!

'... "These are the ones who come out of the great tribulation, and washed their robes and made them white in the blood of the Lamb." Revelation 7:14

I remember a heated conversation I had with a respected pastor. He cut me off after I shared the resurrection of overcomers out of the Great Tribulation is in Revelation 7. He scoffed, "You're such a fearmonger. The church is clearly taken up in Chapter 4. You can stay and fight the Beast if you want to. I'll be in heaven celebrating the marriage supper of the Lamb."

"For I testify to everyone who hears the words of the prophecy of this book: If anyone adds to these things, God will add to him the plagues that are written in this book." Revelation 22:18

I was speechless! This pastor had no idea he was adding to the words of this prophecy. There is a promise for those who do. God is going to add to them the plagues written in The Reveation of Jesus Christ.

"And they overcame him by the blood of the Lamb and by the word of their testimony, and they did not love their lives to the death." Revelation 12:11

In the middle of the 70th week, Michael will cast Satan out of heaven for the final time. This is when the Devil will grant his power to the Beast. To avoid being caught during the Great Tribulation of the saints, overcomers won't be able to have a job, a mailing address, even a phone. For many this type of sacrifice will not be a viable option. Why not? Rather than suffer persecution, even martyrdom, many saints will choose to worship the Beast and receive his mark.

'After these things I looked, and behold, a great multitude which no one could number, of all nations, tribes, peoples, and tongues, standing before the throne and before the Lamb, clothed with white robes, with palm branches in their hands, and crying out with a loud voice..." Revelation 7:9-10

As we speak, Watchmen are warning believers to be ready by watching for the events of the six seals. Intercessors are preaching on holiness leading to discernment. Others are exposing popular teachers taking away from The Revelation of Jesus Christ. This is evidence the Holy Spirit is preparing a great multitude to get the victory over the Beast, his image, his mark, and the number of his name. After their deliverance, they will stand before the throne of God and cry out, "Salvation belongs to our God who sits on the throne, and to the Lamb!"

"Remember therefore how you have received and heard; hold fast and repent. Therefore if you will not watch, I will come upon you as a thief, and you will not know what hour I will come upon you." Revelation 3:3

Jesus is exhorting us to remember what we have received and heard concerning His coming. The overcomers identifying the Abomination of Desolation will be ready for the coming of the Son of Man! He will come as a thief for those refusing to watch. "But, Paul, there are no events left to be fulfilled. Why should we watch for the Antichrist? The church will be gone!" Let's be clear, the Christians refusing to watch are not only denying His words, they're disobeying the One they call Lord!

"But why do you call Me 'Lord, Lord,' and not do the things which I say?" Luke 6:46

This is why anyone believing the Beast will never war against the saints is taking away from The Revelation of Jesus Christ.

"Behold, I am coming quickly! Hold fast what you have, that no one may take your crown." Revelation 3:11

Years ago, a celebrated evangelist wanted to see the fruit from his popular crusades. His association used conversion cards submitted at an altar call five years earlier. Of those contacted, a mere one in ten still believed in Jesus. Yet, the thousands praying the sinner's prayer that night were told they're eternally secure. He assured them nothing can ever change this glorious truth. To this preacher, salvation is merely a transaction. To complete it, one only has to accept the offer. The truth is, our Lord Jesus desires a relationship that is much more than our initial acceptance. This is why He is exhorting us to hold fast, continue in the faith, and not let anyone take our crown!

"For true and righteous are His judgments, because He has judged the great Harlot who corrupted the earth with her fornication; and He has avenged on her the blood of His servants shed by her." Revelation 19:2

Two esteemed worship leaders recently joined a praise group at the Vatican. This ecumenical event was deceptively being advertised as a renewal in the Holy Spirit. Several Christian speakers at this vigil admitted there are doctrinal differences between Protestants, Catholics and Jews. Even so, they love the unity they have for each other. Saints, we know the face of our Lord is against those who do evil. There is no unity between the righteous and the unrighteous. What is happening? The voice of the Harlot is deceiving Christians into supporting an interfaith movement promising unity for all people.

'He causes all, both small and great, rich and poor, free and slave, to receive a mark on their right hand or on their foreheads.' Revelation 13:16

As we draw closer to the harvest, more and more pastors are teaching the church will experience the Great Tribulation. What an awesome answer to prayer. The problem is some are not telling the whole truth. They're claiming the saints overcome (deceived) by the Beast will not lose their salvation. In their minds, a saint can never be lost. They're teaching only pretenders can have an evil heart of unbelief departing from the living God. I ask you, how can the wicked forsake a faith they never had? It's shocking to see how ministers can see the truth in one area yet be blinded in another. I ask you, how many will choose to worship the Beast rather than being killed by the False Prophet? It will be an easy choice for those convinced they cannot depart from God.

This is why anyone believing the elect cannot lose their crowns is taking away from The Revelation of Jesus Christ.

'Behold, He is coming with clouds, and every eye will see Him, even they who pierced Him. And all the tribes of the earth will mourn because of Him. Even so, Amen.' Revelation 1:7

'... "Come, I will show you the bride, the Lamb's wife." And he carried me away in the Spirit to a great and high mountain, and showed me the great city, the holy Jerusalem, descending out of heaven from God.' Revelation 21:9-10

Throughout history, most theologians have taught the Second Coming of Christ is a singular event. This is why they insist the coming of the Son of Man and the return of the Lamb of God are the same visit. The truth is the Second Coming has a beginning and an ending. It will begin when every eye will see the Son of Man coming in the clouds. It will end when the Lamb of God returns with His bride. But, Paul, why does it matter? Can't those denying this truth still get the victory over the Beast? Saints, trusting in another popular interpretation that is taking away from The Revelation of Jesus Christ is unacceptable!

'He who testifies to these things says, "Surely I am coming quickly." Amen. Even so, come, Lord Jesus!' Revelation 22:20

Within, The Revelation of Jesus Christ, let's review the four visits our Lord will accomplish during His Second Coming.

His Second Coming will begin between the sixth and seventh seals, after the **Son of Man** sends forth His angels to gather believers before the throne of God.

Between the sixth and seventh trumpets, the **Holy One** will return to fulfill the mystery of God, the salvation of Israel.

After the seventh bowl, the **Word of God** will appear with His armies of angels at the battle of Armageddon and cast the Beast and the False Prophet into the lake of fire.

His Second Coming will end when the **Lamb of God** and His bride descend inside a new heaven to a new earth.

This is why anyone believing the Second Coming is a single visit is taking away from The Revelation of Jesus Christ.

'Blessed is he who reads and those who hear the words of this prophecy, and keep those things which are written in it; for the time is near.' Revelation 1:3

Who will refuse to listen to the Holy Spirit?
It will be those believing the gifts of the Spirit have ceased.

Who will not recognize the Abomination of Desolation?
It will be those believing they will be gone.

Who will receive the mark of the Beast?
It will be those believing they can never lose their crown.

Who will deny the events of His Second Coming?
It will be those believing His Second Coming is one visit.

"...I have made you a watchman for the house of Israel; therefore you shall hear a word from My mouth and warn them for Me." Ezekiel 33:7

Paul, I believe the Holy Spirit is leading me to become a Watchman to the body of Christ. Before I begin this ministry, what foundational truths should I understand?

A capable watchman should be able to scripturally define the Beginning of Sorrows, the Great Tribulation, the Day of the Lord and the 1,000-year reign of Christ. Understanding the events that take place during these four time periods is critical.

The Beginning of Sorrows will begin after the first seal is opened. It will end after the famines, pestilences, and earthquakes from the third seal cease in the middle of the seven-year week.

Discovering the Events of the Second Coming

The Great Tribulation of the saints will begin after the fourth seal is opened. Satan's wrath will end after the sixth seal.

The Day of the Lord will begin with fire after the seventh seal is opened. The wrath of the Lamb will end after the seventh bowl.

Their 1,000-year reign will begin when the Lamb and His bride descend to a new earth. Their rule over the nations will end with the release of Satan and the destruction of the human race.

"...Do not seal the words of the prophecy of this book, for the time is at hand." Revelation 22:10

I believe in these last days, <u>Discovering The Events Of The Second Coming</u> will become a valuable roadmap for many overcomers. This book will also benefit those saved after the resurrection. Like a light shining in darkness, I pray their understanding of the Day of the Lord help them safely navigate past the battle of Armageddon. May the Holy Spirit empower them to reach many sinners during the reign of Christ.

"Behold, I am coming quickly! Blessed is he who keeps the words of the prophecy of this book." Revelation 22:7

Joseph of Arimathea felt the urgency of the hour when he asked for the body of Jesus. As we draw closer to the harvest, what is our urgency? May we never be silenced. Blessed is he who keeps the words of The Revelation of Jesus Christ.

Your Watchman, Paul Bortolazzo

Chart: The Seven Seals

THE SEVEN SEALS
From the signing of the Covenant to the Day of the Lord

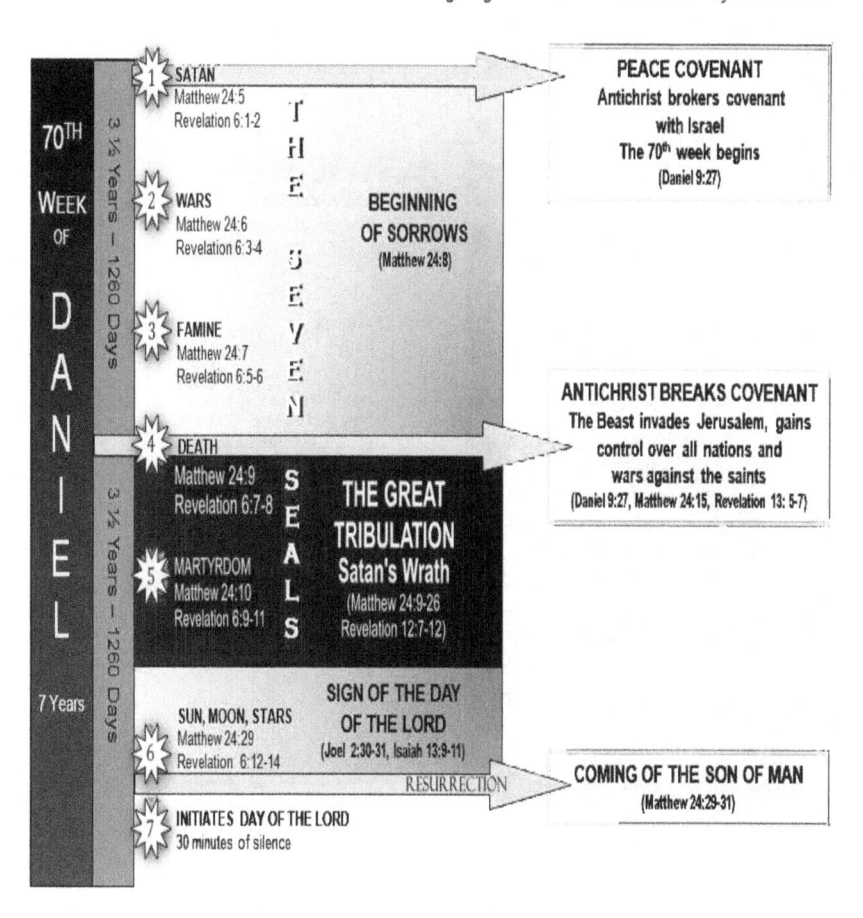

70TH WEEK OF DANIEL — 7 Years
- 3 ½ Years – 1260 Days
- 3 ½ Years – 1260 Days

THE SEVEN SEALS

1. **SATAN** — Matthew 24:5; Revelation 6:1-2
2. **WARS** — Matthew 24:6; Revelation 6:3-4 — *BEGINNING OF SORROWS (Matthew 24:8)*
3. **FAMINE** — Matthew 24:7; Revelation 6:5-6
4. **DEATH** — Matthew 24:9; Revelation 6:7-8
5. **MARTYRDOM** — Matthew 24:10; Revelation 6:9-11

THE GREAT TRIBULATION — Satan's Wrath (Matthew 24:9-26; Revelation 12:7-12)

6. **SUN, MOON, STARS** — Matthew 24:29; Revelation 6:12-14 — *SIGN OF THE DAY OF THE LORD (Joel 2:30-31, Isaiah 13:9-11)*

RESURRECTION

7. **INITIATES DAY OF THE LORD** — 30 minutes of silence

PEACE COVENANT
Antichrist brokers covenant with Israel
The 70th week begins
(Daniel 9:27)

ANTICHRIST BREAKS COVENANT
The Beast invades Jerusalem, gains control over all nations and wars against the saints
(Daniel 9:27, Matthew 24:15, Revelation 13: 5-7)

COMING OF THE SON OF MAN
(Matthew 24:29-31)

Chart: The Second Coming Of Christ

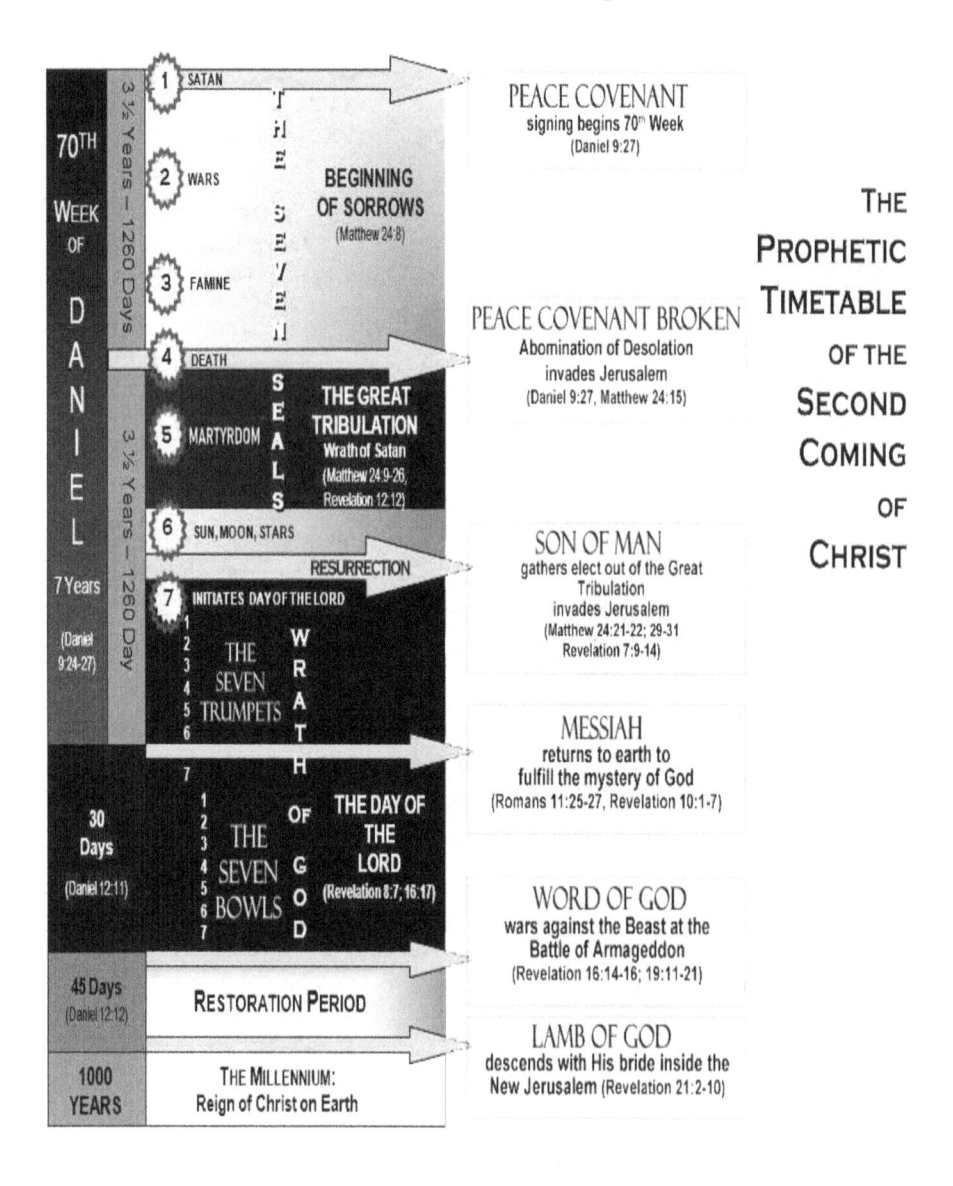

The Prophetic Timetable of the Second Coming of Christ

70TH WEEK OF DANIEL — 7 Years (Daniel 9:24-27)

3½ Years – 1260 Days:
1. SATAN
2. WARS — BEGINNING OF SORROWS (Matthew 24:8)
3. FAMINE

PEACE COVENANT — signing begins 70th Week (Daniel 9:27)

THE SEVEN

3½ Years – 1260 Days:
4. DEATH
5. MARTYRDOM — THE GREAT TRIBULATION — Wrath of Satan (Matthew 24:9-26, Revelation 12:12)
6. SUN, MOON, STARS — RESURRECTION

PEACE COVENANT BROKEN — Abomination of Desolation invades Jerusalem (Daniel 9:27, Matthew 24:15)

SEALS

7. INITIATES DAY OF THE LORD

SON OF MAN gathers elect out of the Great Tribulation invades Jerusalem (Matthew 24:21-22; 29-31 Revelation 7:9-14)

THE SEVEN TRUMPETS — WRATH

MESSIAH returns to earth to fulfill the mystery of God (Romans 11:25-27, Revelation 10:1-7)

30 Days (Daniel 12:11) — THE SEVEN BOWLS — THE DAY OF THE LORD (Revelation 8:7; 16:17) — OF GOD

WORD OF GOD wars against the Beast at the Battle of Armageddon (Revelation 16:14-16; 19:11-21)

45 Days (Daniel 12:12) — RESTORATION PERIOD

LAMB OF GOD descends with His bride inside the New Jerusalem (Revelation 21:2-10)

1000 YEARS — THE MILLENNIUM: Reign of Christ on Earth

Chart: The 70 Weeks of Daniel

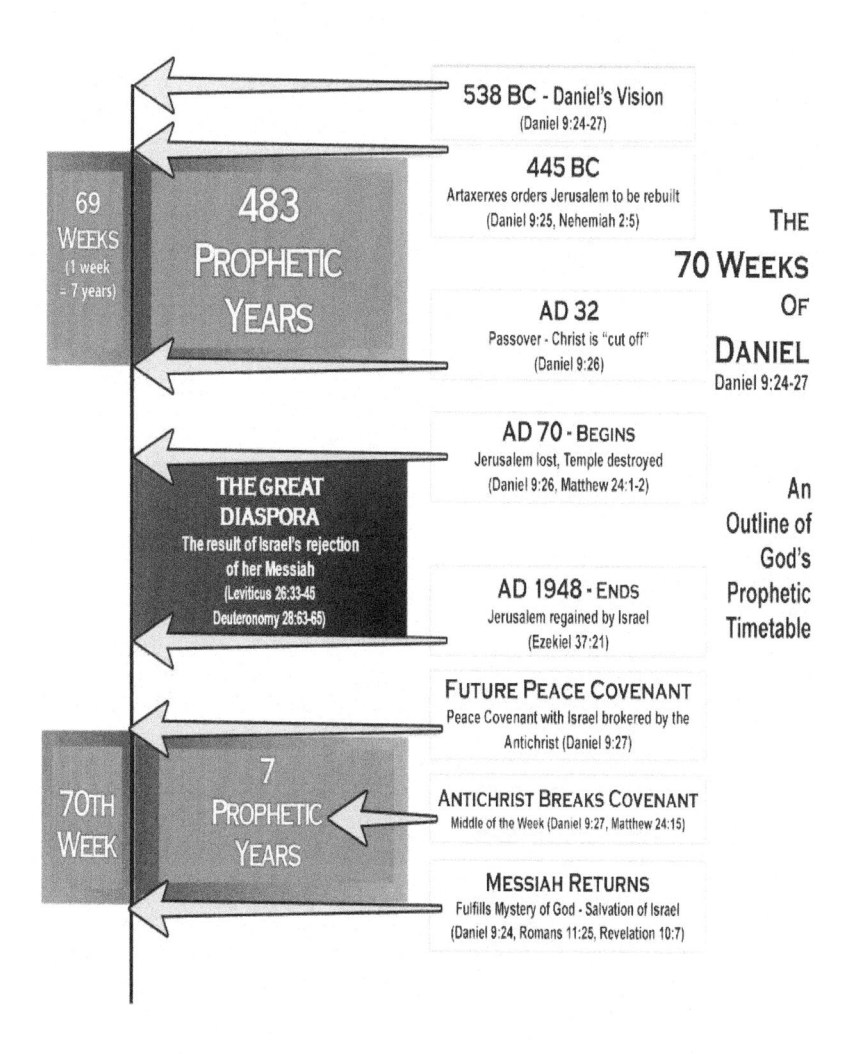

69 WEEKS (1 week = 7 years)

483 PROPHETIC YEARS

538 BC – Daniel's Vision
(Daniel 9:24-27)

445 BC
Artaxerxes orders Jerusalem to be rebuilt
(Daniel 9:25, Nehemiah 2:5)

AD 32
Passover – Christ is "cut off"
(Daniel 9:26)

AD 70 – BEGINS
Jerusalem lost, Temple destroyed
(Daniel 9:26, Matthew 24:1-2)

THE GREAT DIASPORA
The result of Israel's rejection of her Messiah
(Leviticus 26:33-45
Deuteronomy 28:63-65)

AD 1948 – ENDS
Jerusalem regained by Israel
(Ezekiel 37:21)

FUTURE PEACE COVENANT
Peace Covenant with Israel brokered by the Antichrist (Daniel 9:27)

70TH WEEK

7 PROPHETIC YEARS

ANTICHRIST BREAKS COVENANT
Middle of the Week (Daniel 9:27, Matthew 24:15)

MESSIAH RETURNS
Fulfills Mystery of God – Salvation of Israel
(Daniel 9:24, Romans 11:25, Revelation 10:7)

THE **70 WEEKS** OF **DANIEL**
Daniel 9:24-27

An Outline of God's Prophetic Timetable

Made in the USA
Middletown, DE
08 February 2020